Fc
For Fc

+

Quality Assurance in Manufacturing
(Expanded Edition)

Includes New Sections on
Research & Development and Benchmarking

Allison Shearsett and Louis Bevoc

Published by
NutriNiche System LLC

For information contact:
Info@nutriniche.com

Louis Bevoc books...simple explanations of complex subjects

Food Safety	2
Quality Assurance	43
Research & Development	61
Benchmarking	73

Food Safety For Food Processors
A Guide for Implementation

Allison Shearsett and Louis Bevoc

Published by
NutriNiche System LLC

For information contact:
Info@nutriniche.com

Louis Bevoc books...simple explanations of complex subjects

Introduction ... 5
Requirements ... 5
Government agencies ... 5
Food and Drug Administration (FDA) ... 5
United States Department of Agriculture (USDA) ... 8
Center for Disease Control (CDC) ... 8
External factors ... 9
Customer standards ... 9
Customer audits ... 9
Third party audits ... 10
Internal programs ... 10
Good Manufacturing Practices (GMP) ... 10
Sanitation Standard Operating Procedures (SSOP) ... 13
HACCP (Hazard Analysis Critical Control Point) ... 18
Food security ... 25
Pest control ... 27

Allergens ... 29
Soy ... 30
Wheat ... 30
Milk ... 31
Egg ... 32
Fish ... 32
Shellfish ... 33
Peanut ... 33
Tree nut ... 34
Sesame ... 35
Mustard ... 35
Other ... 36
Allergen program ... 36

Recalls ... 38
Health hazards ... 38
Allergens ... 39

Lack of inspection	39
Recall Program	40

Summary 41

Introduction

Most people do not expect to get sick or injured from the food they consume. After, it comes from food manufacturers who are regulated by the government, and those manufacturers operate under rules that protect the public from any type of risk. The problem with this thinking is the fact that it is only partially true. Yes, there are regulations in place for food manufacturers...but those regulations are sometimes bent, broken, misunderstood, or not enforced.

Unfortunately, millions of people are affected each year by some type of foodborne illness. They experience pain, hospital trips, and even death due to food related problems. The worst part about these illnesses is the fact that they could have been prevented if food safety measures had been implemented at the manufacturer, distributor, retailer, and consumer levels.

This book focuses on food safety for food manufacturers (also known as processors). First, it examines requirements imposed by government agencies, customers, and the processors themselves. Next, it looks at biological, chemical, and physical health hazards associated with processing. Then it looks at the impact of allergens on people and processes. Last, but certainly not least in the minds of food processing leaders, it explores food product recalls.

> ***Note: Text that is bold-italicized shows examples that could be used in food processing plants. These examples are not complete, but they have real-world application.***

Now that you understand the scope of this book, let's move into the ways that food safety controls are established at the manufacturing level. To do this, food safety requirements are discussed in the next section.

Requirements

Food processors have many rules in place for food safety. These rules regulate processes, procedures, and people in workplaces to make sure the products produced are safe for human consumption. These rules are established by:

Government agencies

Like they do for most other industries, the government oversees many different aspects of food processing. Regulations dictate what food processors can and cannot do, and most of those regulations are based on making sure the food produced is safe for people to eat.

The three major government overseers discussed in this book are the Food and Drug Administration (FDA), United States Department of Agriculture (USDA), and Center for Disease Control (CDC). Below is a description of the roles that these organizations play regarding food safety.

Food and Drug Administration (FDA)

The FDA oversees the bulk of food manufactured in the United States. Their role is to protect the public by establishing and enforcing food safety rules and regulations. They ally with state and local authorities to make the overall food safety system better and stronger.

The following is a general list of FDA responsibilities:

- Food (other than most egg, meat, and poultry)
- Food additives
- Beverages (water, milk, beer, soda, wine, etc.)
- Dietary supplements (vitamins, minerals, etc.)
- infant formulas

In its capacity, the FDA works to prevent food safety issues from occurring. They do this by requiring food processors to write food safety plans designed to identify food safety hazards that are likely to occur. Once those hazards are identified, controls need to be put in place to minimize them. These controls need to be monitored, and failures must be addressed with correction actions and preventative measures.

The following is an example of how a food safety hazard is addressed for a candy company:

Food safety hazard

> Metal could get into the product during processing. This metal could come from broken equipment or machinery, and it could also come in with the raw materials (chocolate, sugar, honey, nuts, etc.)

Controls

> Metal detection will be on every production line at the time of packaging for each box of product.

Monitoring of controls

> Test wands made of ferrous, non-ferrous, and stainless steel will be put through the metal detectors every two hours to make sure they are working properly. If the metal detector does not detect the wands and shut down the line, then it is not working properly.

Corrective action

> If a metal detector is found to not be functioning properly, then the line will be stopped until the problem is resolved and the unit is functioning correctly. Additionally, if the metal detector is found not to be working properly, all products back to the last acceptable check will be retained and run through the machine again once it is working properly.

The above example identifies the hazard as metal. It then incorporates metal detection as a control and monitors that control with test wands containing three common types of metal. If the metal detector fails to recognize any of these metals, then it is repaired and all products up to the last acceptable check are re-run through it.

Unfortunately, food safety plans do not always work as intended. If the plan is not effective, then the public gets contaminated or adulterated product. If news of this contamination reaches the FDA, then they will take action. Depending on the severity of the situation, the FDA can mandate a recall of the affected product (recalls are discussed in more detail later in this book).

The following is an example of how this happens using the candy company:

> A customer buys a box of caramel chocolate candy and breaks a tooth eating a piece. She knows she bit down on something hard and, upon examination, finds that it is a piece of hard plastic.
>
> The customer contacts the manager at the store where she bought the product. The manager contacts the FDA to report the incident, and the FDA sends an inspector to the candy plant to begin an investigation.
>
> With the inspector's help, the candy company discovers that a piece of the plastic paddle used for mixing the caramel is missing. They look at their documentation and find that maintenance last recorded the paddles were in proper working order three weeks ago. They also know that caramel is used in three different types of chocolates.
>
> Based on the information the candy company has available, they initiate a recall for all three chocolate candies that contain caramel. The recall includes any product made over the last three weeks since that was the last documented check of the condition of the paddles.
>
> In this case, the candy company voluntarily conducted a recall. Their documentation supported the amount of product recalled, so the FDA did not need to mandate any action. They merely acted as an overseer of the recall process.

The FDA also has the authority to stop production at a food processor if they witness or have reason to believe that product has been intentionally adulterated. Food can be purposefully contaminated by competitors, disgruntled employees, or the general public for a variety of different reasons...and the FDA gets involved when this happens.

All processing records concerning food safety must be available to FDA inspection personnel upon request. They are authorized to make decisions based upon those records, and those decisions can be as severe as shutting down plants until product is considered safe for human consumption or corrective action is taken. Along the same lines, they can send products out for laboratory testing if processing records indicate they are adulterated in any way.

Contrary to what some people believe, the FDA also offers support to food processors. Inspectors understand government rules and regulations better than most people, and they can help managers of plants avoid pitfalls by offering simple advice. However, that advice must be limited because "consulting" by FDA inspectors is considered a conflict of interest that can jeopardize their Jobs.

United States Department of Agriculture (USDA)

The USDA oversees the bulk of meat, poultry, and egg products manufactured in the United States. They ensure that these products are safe, wholesome, and properly labeled following the same basic rules and regulations used by the FDA.

The USDA differs from the FDA for the following reasons:

- USDA issues establishment numbers for every processing facility and these numbers must be listed on every product along with the USDA mark of inspection (also known as an inspection legend). In general, FDA products do not require inspection legends or establishment numbers on finished products.
- USDA makes HACCP plans mandatory for all processing plants, and every product manufactured in those facilities must fall under those plans. This is not the case for all FDA processing plants.
- USDA has an everyday presence in the processing facilities that they regulate. The FDA is only present periodically or when needed due to food safety concerns.
- USDA requires approval of every product label from its labeling division. FDA does not require label approval.
- The USDA routinely samples products from every processing plant for pathogenic bacteria. Products from FDA processing plants are not routinely sampled.
- USDA and FDA have similar (and often the same) rules regarding food safety, but USDA plants are monitored more rigorously due to the fact the products being manufactured (meat, poultry, and eggs) are a higher risk for food safety.

Center for Disease Control (CDC)

The CDC provides a link between government agencies (FDA and USDA) and foodborne illnesses of consumers. They do this by tracking bacteria patterns (also known as DNA fingerprints) that identify outbreaks and pinpoint the sources of problems. The public can then be warned about avoiding these sources, and the government can begin procedures for containment and eradication.

The following is an example of the CDC in action:

A bacteria outbreak linked to milk sickens over 100 people in Michigan, Ohio, and Indiana. The CDC uses DNA fingerprinting to identify three rare strains of the E. coli that are closely related in terms of genetics.

This information leads investigators to look for a single source of the outbreak. They analyze milk samples from several different organizations and, by process of elimination, determine that source is a farm in Indiana.

CDC stops the farm from selling milk, and the public is warned about the E .coli problem associated with it. Dairy processors determine the products that utilized this milk, and a recall is put into effect.

The above example is similar to a real situation that occurred with cheese, and it shows how the CDC is able to attach foodborne illness to specific products and settings. They work to find, investigate, and control bacterial outbreaks before sickness spreads to large numbers of people.

External factors

The government plays a major role in making sure food processors produce safe products for people to eat. However, many other people are involved with food safety…and their roles are often just as important.

The following are examples of external factors that dictate food safety procedures for food processors:

Customer standards

Some customers have specific standards they want to be followed. For example, they might require that certain pieces of equipment are checked throughout the day for missing parts, or they require X-ray instead of metal detection. Many of these standards stem from problems customers have had in the past. They do not want these problems to reoccur, so they demand preventative food safety measures for the companies that manufacture their products.

Customer audits

Some customers conduct audits of the companies that manufacture their food products. These audits are performed by employees of the customers whose purpose is to make sure processors have food safety procedures in place.

Customer audits are commonly referred to as second-party audits. They are often based on written food safety agreements that have been established. Customers want to verify that processors are adhering to the specified requirements, so they conduct audits of those processors' facilities.

Third party audits

Third party audits are similar to customer audits except they are conducted by an independent third party. Typically these third parties are experienced auditors of food processing plants, and they target specific aspects of food safety.

Customers often request third party audits when they do not have the necessary in-house resources to conduct them or they want a non-bias professional review. Sometimes they want food processors to meet certain standards that can be verified by the third party. Other times they want food processors to achieve some type of certification that can be issued by the third party.

Internal programs

These programs are the heart of food safety. They are developed and implemented by the processors, and they are used by the government and auditors as support that food safety systems are in place and working as designed.

Important internal programs include:

Good Manufacturing Practices (GMP)

Food safety is arguably the most important aspect of food processing today. Every food plant management team must have some knowledge of the subject or they risk recall, temporary shutdown, and even loss of their business. This leads to a very good question. Where does the food processing owner or manager begin? The answer is Good Manufacturing Practices or GMPs. Without GMPs, food plants would certainly be at risk for sanitation and hygiene issues that lead to food safety problems.

GMPs are part of the foundation for a good food safety program. They help prevent food adulteration, food contamination (physical, chemical, and biological) and unsanitary processing conditions. A plethora of problems including wasted production time, shortened shelf life, spoilage, and recall can be avoided by adhering to GMPs. In other words, GMPs can keep a food plant out of a lot of trouble.

Planning is the key to developing good GMPs. When it comes to food safety, an ounce of prevention truly is worth a pound of cure. Plant management should implement specific policies so wholesome products can be manufactured. Written procedures should be distributed to employees, posted in conspicuous areas, and kept in an official file.

Training should be conducted to incorporate the GMP procedures and answer related questions. This training needs to be conducted in two parts:

Orientation

Employees should be trained before they start working. This prepares them for the jobs they are about to perform and eliminates the time and money issues involved with pulling employees off production lines. In short, management needs to meet with all new employees and review the organization's established GMPs to avoid the violation of those GMPs.

Annual

Employees should be trained every year to implement updates, answer questions, and refresh memories. In addition to lectures, filming, or videotaping employees doing their actual jobs can help accomplish this. Keep the footage brief...maybe 10 to 15 minutes. Point out when GMPs are being adhered to or violated using praise and constructive criticism. People tend to pay a great deal to a video or DVD that they personally appear in.

Many GMPs are listed in the United States Food and Drug Administration (FDA) regulations. These regulations address employees, plants, equipment, and processes for the manufacturing of many food products. They can be tailored to fit the specific needs of a wide variety of food processing plants.

This book cannot list good manufacturing practices for every type of food processor, but the following are some examples of simple GMPs that could be incorporated into a bakery:

1. **Disease Control**

    a. *Employees with open sores, infected wounds, or other microbial contamination will not work in production areas if contact with food or a food contact surface is reasonably likely to occur.*
    b. *Illnesses will be reported to plant management, and doctor's notes may be required before being allowed to return to work.*

2. **Cleanliness and Personal Hygiene**

    a. *Company supplied coats will be worn in all processing areas.*
    b. *Hands and/or gloves (of an impermeable material) will be washed and sanitized before entering production areas and anytime they become contaminated.*
    c. *Jewelry is not allowed, and rings will be covered by gloves.*
    d. *Hair nets will be worn by all personnel so that all hair is restrained, and beard nets will be worn when growth is exhibited.*
    e. *Personal items will not be stored in production areas.*
    f. *Eating, drinking, spitting, chewing gum, and smoking will not be allowed in production areas.*

3. **Plant and Grounds**

    a. Equipment will be stored so grounds can be properly maintained.
    b. Weeds adjacent to the building will be cut to discourage rodent harborage.
    c. Grounds will drain to prevent pooling and potential breeding ground for pests.
    d. Waste will be disposed of in a manner that discourages contamination.
    e. Plant design and construction will facilitate sanitary operations and prevent pest infestation.
    f. Lighting will be adequate for employees to perform the visual aspect of their job functions
    g. Safety-type light bulbs and/or coverings will be used to prevent glass breakage.
    h. Ventilation will be adequate so the growth of pathogenic organisms and pests are not promoted.

4. Sanitary Operations

    a. Equipment will be disassembled, cleaned, and sanitized as needed to protect food against contamination.
    b. Food contact surfaces and non-food contact surfaces will be cleaned and sanitized as needed to protect food against contamination.
    c. Cleaning and sanitizing of equipment and food contact surfaces will follow instructions on container labels.
    d. Pesticides, insecticides, and/or rodenticides will be applied by licensed professionals using caution to protect against food contamination.

5. Sanitary Facilities and Controls

    a. All water will be potable (clean and suitable for drinking). This includes water used for processing, cleaning, and making ice.
    b. Hot water (130F minimum) will be provided for washing hands and/or equipment.
    c. Sewage and disposable waste will be properly conveyed from the facility.
    d. Sanitary and properly maintained toilet facilities and welfare areas will be provided for all employees.
    e. Signs directing employees to wash hands will be prominently displayed where appropriate
    f. Trash receptacles will be designed to prevent harborage for pests and rodents, and those receptacles will not contact food.

6. Equipment and utensils

    a. Equipment and utensils will be designed for easy cleaning

b. Equipment will be designed for protection against food contamination
c. Equipment and utensils will be properly maintained
d. Food contact surfaces will be corrosion resistant
e. Instrumentation used to control critical parameters (pH, temperature, etc.,) will be calibrated and accurate.
f. Coolers and freezers will be fitted with thermometers for temperature monitoring.

7. Processes and Controls

    a. Raw materials and other food ingredients (liquid or dry) will be inspected at receiving and during production to ensure they are wholesome and suitable for processing. Specifically, employees will look for physical, biological, and chemical hazards. Letters of guarantee, along with chemical and microbiological specifications (meeting FDA standards for safe human consumption where applicable) will be available from all suppliers and may be requested if non-compliance is suspected.
    b. Packaging materials will be inspected at receiving and during productions to ensure they are in good condition. Letters of guarantee will be available from all suppliers and may be requested if conditions warrant the need.

        (1) Packaging materials will be received and stored in a manner designed to protect against physical, chemical, and biological contamination.

        (2) Packaging materials will be properly rotated using a First-in, first-out (FIFO) inventory method.

    g. Processing will be conducted under conditions that minimize physical, chemical, and microbiological contamination.
    h. Food production areas and machinery will not be used for nonhuman food-grade products (pet food, animal feed, etc.).

8. Warehousing and distribution

    a. Storage and transportation of finished product will protect the food from physical, chemical, and biological contamination.
    b. Natural and/or unavoidable defects that present no health hazards will remain within FDA established limits.

Now you understand the basic concept of GMPs, let's move into the next section that addresses sanitation in food plants...better known as SSOPs.

Sanitation Standard Operating Procedures (SSOP)

SSOPs differ from GMPs because the focus is on sanitation. GMPs should be taken into account when incorporating SSOPs into a processing plant's food safety program, but SSOPs detail sanitation tasks.

Essentially, SSOPs should address:

(1) The description of the task
(2) The purpose of the task
(3) The frequency of the task
(4) The individual(s) responsible for performing the task
(5) The procedure for performing the task (list all steps)
(6) The corrective action taken if the task is not properly completed

SSOPs are published in the Code of Federal Regulations. It states, "Each official establishment shall develop, implement, and maintain written standard operating procedures for sanitation (Sanitation SOP's)." Most meat and poultry plants refer to this section for the implementation of SSOPs, but the general concept can be applied to all food processing plants.

First, the SSOP must be developed. Clear and concise procedures that prevent adulteration and contamination need to be written. Excessive wording often makes understanding and performing tasks more difficult. These procedures should list actions to be taken before and during processing on every day the plant operates.

An example of a pre-operational procedure is as follows:

> *A pre-operational inspection will be conducted by a designated employee every day before production start-up. Deficiencies and corrections will be noted on the pre-operational log, and food contact surface deficiencies will be discussed with the sanitation manager.*

An example of an operational procedure is as follows:

> *Product will be removed from coolers under the direction of the sanitation supervisor before any cleaning of floors, walls, or ceilings begins. Any product coming in direct contact with cleaning chemicals will be condemned and put in inedible.*

A responsible individual with the authority to make decisions for sanitation related issues should sign the SSOP upon implementation, anytime the program is modified, and once a year for reassessment. Her or his signature signifies that the establishment is adhering to the procedures outlined in the program.

An example of a change is the following:

> *On June 20, 2016, foaming sanitizers were removed from all finished product entrances. A dry quat known to kill Listeria will now be used.*

Signed:_____   Date:_____

An example of a reassessment is the following:

> *On May 14, 2016, our SSOP program was reassessed and found to be acceptable.*

Signed:_____   Date:_____

SSOPs should be continuously evaluated for effectiveness, even if the evaluations are not documented. Ineffective SSOPs often result in governmental intervention, which can make things much more difficult for everyone involved.

Prevention is the key to good SSOPs. Always remember to design SSOP plans that work and are feasible. Do not simply write something because it "looks good" on paper. Plants are held accountable for the plans they develop, so be sure that the personnel performing the tasks can follow everything that is written.

Corrective actions are also important. Corrective actions must (1) restore sanitary conditions, (2) ensure proper product disposition if necessary, and (3) prevent reoccurrence of the contamination or adulteration. Improvements or modifications to the existing SSOPs should also be detailed and documented.

Examples of sufficient and insufficient corrective action for a vegetable-slicing blade found to be improperly cleaned during preoperational inspection include:

Insufficient corrective action

> *The blade was cleaned.*

Sufficient corrective action:

> *The blade was removed, cleaned, and sanitized at 5:40 am. No product was involved. This problem will be discussed with our sanitation supervisor, and the responsible employee will be verbally reinstructed on proper cleaning of the slicer to avoid reoccurrence.*

Record keeping should be maintained to document the implementation and monitoring of SSOPs and corrective actions. Employees responsible for implementing and monitoring specific procedures should initial and date those procedures daily.

Records can be computerized or handwritten. These records must be (1) maintained for a minimum of two years and (2) made available for government agencies' review within 24 hours of the request.

FDA and USDA inspection personnel will verify an establishment's SSOP program periodically or when they feel it is necessary to verify effectiveness and adequacy. This verification includes:

(1) A general review of SSOP records
(2) An analysis of SSOP procedures and corrective actions
(3) Direct observation of the SSOP procedures specified
(4) Microbiological testing to access sanitary conditions

Keep in mind that supporting documentation is very important for establishing the effectiveness of an SSOP program...and history provides good supporting documentation. If a plant can show that established procedures have been successful over a period of time, then there will likely be less intervention by governmental inspection personnel.

Some essential components of SSOPs have been discussed. The following is an excerpt from a basic SSOP program that might be written for a dairy processing plant:

> *The sanitation manager will be responsible for implementing the SSOPs. Designated quality control employees will conduct pre-operational and operational inspection procedures. Any problems or deficiencies found will be documented, responsible employees will be notified, and corrective action will be administered.*
>
> *All soaps, sanitizers, and cleaners are stored in non-production areas, and they will be used per manufacturer recommendations and OSHA guidelines. All water used in the plant is potable. The term "washed" refers to the use of hot water only. The term "cleaned" refers to the use of hot water, soap, and sanitizer being used in the process. Sanitizers do not require rinsing.*
>
> *1. Raw Product Processing Areas*
>
> > *a. All machines will be disassembled (where possible) after each day's production. Residue will be removed by hand and put in inedible. Food contact surfaces will be cleaned (heavily soiled areas will be scrubbed with brushes). Nonfood contact Surfaces will be washed and/or cleaned*
> > *b. Utensils, knives, hand tools, lugs, and tables will be cleaned after each day's production.*
> > *c. Floors and walls will be cleaned after each day's production.*
> > *d. Drain baskets will be emptied in inedible containers and drains will be cleaned after each day's production.*
> > *e. Trash will be disposed of in designated, non-processing areas.*
> > *f. Condensation will be wiped when present and problems will be documented.*
> > *g. Problems resulting in potential contamination or adulteration of product will be immediately corrected or production will stop in the affected areas until the problem is corrected. All sanitation*

problems will be documented and discussed with sanitation personnel.

2. Finished Product Processing Areas

   a. All machines will be disassembled (where possible) after each day's production. Residue will be removed by hand and put in inedible. Food Contact Surfaces will be cleaned (heavily soiled areas will be scrubbed with brushes). Non-food contact surfaces will be washed and/or cleaned
   b. Utensils, knives, hand tools, lugs, and tables will be cleaned after each day's production.
   c. Floors and walls will be cleaned after each day's production.
   d. Drain baskets will be emptied in inedible containers and drains will be cleaned after each day's production.
   e. Trash will be disposed of in designated, non-processing areas.
   f. Maintenance personnel will wear designated color coats distinguishable from those worn by production employees when working on packaging machinery. Contact surfaces on machines will be sanitized after work is performed if that work affects those surfaces.
   g. When using hoses, care will be taken to assure that water is not splashed on any already cleaned and sanitized machines or equipment. Sanitized machines or equipment splashed with water will be re-cleaned and re-sanitized.
   h. Condensation will be wiped when present and problems will be documented.
   i. Problems resulting in potential contamination or adulteration of product will be immediately corrected or production will stop in the affected areas until the problem is corrected. All sanitation problems will be documented and discussed with sanitation personnel.

3. ADDITIONAL AREAS

   a. Refrigeration Units

      1. Unit pan will be cleaned
      2. Coils and fins will be cleaned
      3. Fan guards will be cleaned

   b. Floors

      1. Dry material will be swept and put in trash or inedible
      2. Floors will be cleaned
      3. Drains will be scrubbed and cleaned

   c. Ceilings and Walls

1. *Residue or debris will be rinsed off*
   2. *Ceilings and walls will be cleaned (and scrubbed if necessary)*

   d. **Reoccurring problems will be discussed with responsible employees and management. Employees will be re-instructed in proper cleaning methodology if necessary.**

Now you have a general idea of what encompasses an SSOP program for a food processing plant. Next, let's move into HACCP…a program that was developed specifically for food safety.

HACCP (Hazard Analysis Critical Control Point)

HACCP refers to written programs that define procedures for food safety. They control biological, chemical, and physical hazards throughout processes in food manufacturing facilities. When effectively implemented, they prevent consumers from becoming ill or, in more serious cases, dying.

Food safety hazards are defined as follows:

Biological

> This hazard results when disease-causing organisms enter food and pose a health threat to consumers. These organisms can be introduced at any time during processing, but they are often a result of poor handling, inadequate sanitation, or cross contamination.
>
> The most common biological hazards are bacteria, but viruses and parasites also fall into this category. Each one of these is described below:
>
> **Bacteria**
>
> Pathogenic bacteria are the major enemy of food processors. They are responsible for a wide variety of food safety issues, and they often lead to production stoppages and recalls.
>
> Some common bacteria that are associated with foodborne illness include:
>
> - Bacillus cereus
> - Campylobacter jejuni
> - Clostridium botulinum
> - Clostridium perfringens
> - Escherichia coli 0157: H7

- Listeria monocytogenes
- Salmonella spp.
- Staphylococcus aureus

Viruses

Viruses insert themselves into host cells and alter the way those cells function. Unlike bacteria, viruses cannot survive without their living hosts. However, similar to bacteria, they can be very pathogenic and infectious.

Some common viruses that are associated with foodborne illness include:

- Bacteriophage
- Hepatitis A virus
- Norovirus
- Norwalk virus

Parasites

Similar to viruses, parasites grow in host organisms. However, unlike viruses, they do not supply their hosts with anything beneficial for survival...so their hosts tend to perish in relatively short periods of time.

Some common viruses that are associated with foodborne illness include:
- Cryptosporidium parvum
- Taenia spp.
- Toxoplasma gondii
- Trichinella spiralis
- Entamoeba coli

Chemical

This hazard results when chemicals enter food and pose a health threat to consumers. These chemicals can be introduced at any time during processing, but they are often a result of poor use or handling. Chemical contaminants can make people very sick, and that is why OSHA Safety Data Sheets (SDS) are required to list first aid procedures for ingestion.

Some common chemicals that are associated with foodborne illness include:

- Cleaning chemicals (soaps, sanitizers, cleaners)
- Maintenance chemicals (oil, gas, lubricants)

- The environment (air, water, earth)
- Food Additives (liquid, solid)
- Pesticides (sprays, liquids, pellets, blocks)

Physical

This hazard results when extraneous materials enter food and pose a health threat to consumers. These materials can be introduced at any time during processing, but they are often a result of poor handling or improper processing. Physical contaminants can cause choking, and they can damage people's mouths, teeth, and internal organs.

Some common chemicals that are associated with foodborne illness include:

- Cardboard
- Dirt
- Fingernails (fake or real)
- Glass
- Hair
- Metal
- Paper
- Plastic
- Stones
- Wood

The best way to describe a HACCP program is to define and exemplify the seven basic principles. These principles are as follows:

Principle 1: Perform a hazard analysis

Food processors need to determine the biological, chemical, and physical hazards that cause food to be unsafe and then identify preventive measures that will control those hazards. Every step in the process, from receiving to shipping, needs to be analyzed for food safety hazards. This analysis looks at the potential for each hazard to occur and determines if that potential is significant. If the potential is significant, then a measure for preventing it from occurring must be designated.

The example below shows three steps in the hazard analysis of a meat processing plant that manufactures ready-to-eat ham products:

FULLY COOKED, READY-TO-EAT
Ham

Ingredient/ Process Step	Potential hazard introduced, controlled or enhanced at this point	Is the potential food safety hazard significant?	Justification for decision	What control measures can be applied to prevent significant hazards?	Is this step a critical control point (CCP)?
SOAK CASINGS	B: Pathogens (Listeria, E. coli, Salmonella)	B: No	B: Low risk. Water is potable and contamination from soaking is unlikely.		B: No
	C: Contamination from cleaning agents or sanitizers	C: No	C: Low risk. GMP addresses storage of chemicals in non-processing areas, and all sanitizers are no rinse and follow container instructions.		C: No
	P: Foreign objects (metal, plastic, wood)	P: No	P: Low risk. Past history (one year) does not indicate contamination problems.		P: No
HANG ON RACKS	B: Pathogens (Listeria, E. coli, Salmonella)	B: No	B. Low risk. Products are stuffed in coolers below 40F. Cooler temperatures are monitored on GMP log		B: No
	C: Contamination from cleaning agents or sanitizers.	C: No	C: Low risk. GMP addresses storage of chemicals in non-processing areas, and all sanitizers are no rinse and follow container instructions.		C: No
	P: Foreign objects (metal, plastic, wood)	P: No	P: Low risk. Visually monitored by de-boning		P: No

			personnel, and past history (one year) does not indicate contamination problems.			
COOK	B: Pathogens (Listeria, Salmonella, and E. coli)	B: Yes	B: Finished Ham is considered ready-to-eat and Listeria, Salmonella, and E. coli could survive if lethality is not reached.	B: Proper finished internal temperature to reduce the risk of pathogen survival.	B: Yes – CCP B1	
	C: None identified (product is in an enclosed smokehouse with contact limited to the smokehouse person)	C: None identified	C: None required		C: No	
	P: None identified (product is in an enclosed smokehouse with contact limited to the smokehouse person)	P: None identified	P: None required		P: No	

In the above example, the first two processing steps (soak casings and hang on racks) do not present a biological, chemical, or physical hazard. However, the third step (cook) presents a biological hazard since Listeria, Salmonella, and E. coli (all three are pathogenic or disease causing bacteria) could survive if the proper temperature is not reached. Based on this potential, cooking is a critical control point (CCP). Critical control points are discussed in more detail in principle two.

Principle 2: Designate critical control points (CCPs)

Critical control points (CCPs) occur at steps in processing where controls can be used to prevent food safety hazards or reduce them to acceptable levels. For example, some foods need to reach a certain pH to be safe, while other foods need to be dried to a certain level (water activity) to be safe.

In the ham processing example, a critical control point occurs at the cook step. If the ham does not reach a certain temperature, then there is a reasonable risk that it might be safe to eat due to Listeria, Salmonella, and E.

coli. Cooking can eliminate these pathogens and reduce the risk to an acceptable level.

Principle 3: Establish critical limits

Critical limits for the CCP need to be established. In other words, maximum and/or minimum values must be implemented so the CCP is effective in eliminating the risk or reducing it to an acceptable level.

In the ham processing example, the critical limit implement involves temperature. Specifically, all ham must be cooked to 160F minimum internal temperature. Listeria, Salmonella, and E. coli cannot survive at 160F, so the risk is reduced to an acceptable level.

Principle 4: Establish monitoring requirements

Monitoring requirements of the CCP need to be established. Monitoring is the actual performing of the CCP that keeps the designated food safety hazard(s) from occurring.

In the ham processing example, a designated employee uses a calibrated temperature to establish that the internal temperature of the visibly largest ham on each rack of product is at least 160F.

Principle 5: Establish corrective actions

Corrective actions describe the action that will be taken when monitoring activities exceed established critical limits. This action ensures that contaminated or adulterated product does not reach consumers.

In the ham processing example, all parts of 417.3 (corrective action) in Directive 5000.1 will be addressed. Specifically, this states:

> *(1) The cause of the deviation is identified and eliminated*
> *(2) The CCP will be under control after the corrective action is taken*
> *(3) Measures to prevent recurrence are established*
> *(4) No product that is injurious to health or otherwise adulterated as a result of the deviation enters commerce.*

Principle 6: Establish record keeping requirements

Records that are important to the HACCP plan need to be documented and maintained. These records pertain to the CCP, and they are used as support for the HACCP program. Deviations and corrective actions should also be listed on these records.

In the ham processing example, cooking logs and thermometer calibration logs are the records that need to be documented and maintained. Cooking logs record the finished temperatures of the ham and thermometer calibration logs indicate the thermometers used to take the temperatures are accurate.

Principle 7: Establish verification and validation

This principle has two parts. The first part is verification, and the second part is validation. Both of these are ongoing processes, but verification is done more frequently than validation. Verification is also documented in the HACCP program, while this is not typically the case for validation.

The following is a description of both parts:

Verification

Verification entails observing the monitoring activities and reviewing the records. This confirms that the monitoring activities are following those specified in the HACCP plan, and it assures the records are accurate.

In the ham processing example, quality control personnel verify the monitoring activities weekly to assure they are meeting those specified. Specifically, they watch the monitoring employee to assure the minimum internal temperature reached is 160F and the largest piece of ham on every rack has the temperature taken. The cooking logs and thermometer calibration logs are also reviewed weekly to assure that they are accurate and complete.

Validation

Validation ensures that the HACCP plan is doing what it is designed to do. In other words, is it working properly to prevent the food safety hazard(s) from occurring? The type of action taken and the frequency of that action need to be documented.

In the ham processing example, validation is accomplished by sending finished product out to a lab for microbial analysis every year. This is written as follows:

> ***Once a year a ham will be sent to an accredited laboratory and analyzed for Listeria, Salmonella, and E. coli. Negative results indicate the plan is working, and positive results will require a plan reassessment.***

Below is the HACCP plan for the ham processing example. The table lists every principle discussed above.

Product Category	Process Step	CCP	CCP Description	Critical Limits	Monitoring	Corrective Action	HACCP Records	HACCP System Verification
Ham	Cook	CCP B1	Survival of pathogens (Listeria, Salmonella and E. coli)	Internal meet a minimum of 160F	Monitoring employee takes the internal temperature of the visibly largest piece of ham on every rack using a calibrated hand held thermometer.	Quality Control will address all parts of 417.3 (corrective action) in Directive 5000.1.	Cooking logs and thermometer calibration logs are on file.	Monitoring activities are observed once per week. Quality control employee initials indicate monitoring procedures are acceptable as outlined in the HACCP plan. Records (cooking logs and thermometer calibration logs) are reviewed once per week. Quality control employee initials indicate records are complete and accurate.

Now you understand the basics of a food safety HACCP plan. This leads us to food security...another program essential for assuring unsafe product does not reach consumers.

Food security

Food security programs protect food from tampering, contamination, or other forms of adulteration. They do this by preventing unauthorized personnel from gaining access to food or water supplies and by providing plans for emergencies. In short, they list current controls in place, and outline strategies for catastrophes.

The following is an excerpt from a basic food security program that might be written for a frozen dinner processing plant:

1. ***Controls currently in place include:***

- A. *Employee only entrance – Production employees must enter the building through one door, and visitors are not allowed to enter the building through this door. Any visitor seen at this entrance throws up a red flag and questions are asked as to why this person is at our establishment.*
- B. *Sign-in sheet at visitor's entrance – all visitors must sign in and identify their company and the person they want to meet with.*
- C. *Alarmed points throughout the plant – The alarm system has many checkpoints that monitor the facility when employees are not in the building.*
- D. *Fenced premises– fenced areas are locked and a guard allows access.*
- E. *Cameras with monitors at all entrances – plant entrances (and some processing areas) are continually monitored.*
- F. *Limited roof access – only one door leads to the roof.*
- G. *Exterior lighting - lights the entire building.*
- H. *Backflow devices are on all processing water outlets.*
- I. *Trucks are examined by receiving personnel for defects and foreign material.*
- J. *All raw materials are inspected at the receiving dock.*
- K. *Product coolers are locked when production ends.*
- L. *Designated people have keys and lock doors after production.*
- M. *Product inventories are monitored and recorded by designated personnel.*

2. **Potential Contamination and Action Taken**

   A. Power Failure

   1. Communication via cell phones.
   2. Provide management personnel with flashlights
   3. Determine if the building should be evacuated
   4. Check for trapped people in all areas (processing areas, elevators, stairways, etc.)
   5. Call emergency contacts as determined necessary (refrigeration contractor, electrician, electric and gas company, etc.)
   6. Conduct an onsite inspection to determine if the problem is in our location only, and if not, try to find out when power will be restored
   7. Shut down all equipment that could be damaged when power is restored
   8. Cover exposed product and keep all refrigerator and freezer doors closed
   9. Document all injuries/incidents/expenses incurred

   B. Severe Weather/Tornado

1. Provide flashlights to management personnel
2. Monitor the weather through some channel of communication (radio, television, internet, etc.)
3. Locate safe areas of the building (areas away from glass and windows) for harborage if necessary.
4. Announce status or updates over the page system if necessary
5. Cover exposed product and keep all refrigerator and freezer doors closed
6. Keep in constant communication via cell phones
7. Document all injuries/incidents/expenses incurred

C. Water Contamination

1. Stop all production and cleaning where water is used
2. Locate all product exposed to the contaminated water and retain pending laboratory analysis
3. Used bottled water (or boiled water if possible) for any processing or consumption.
4. After the problem is resolved, flush all lines for 10 minutes and then rinse, wash, and sanitize all food contact surfaces.
5. Document all findings

D. Product Contamination

1. Stop production in the affected area
2. Refer to the HACCP plan for determining if the contamination specifics (chemical, physical, or biological hazard)
3. Identify potential witnesses
4. Consider product laboratory analysis
5. Issue a product recall if necessary
6. Document all findings

Pest control

Pest control programs are implemented to stop pests from entering food processing facilities (rats, mice, birds, etc.) or kill pests once they have entered the building (flies, mosquitoes, roaches, etc.). The major two major categories of these programs are rodent control and pest control.

The following is a description of both categories:

Rodent control

These are the most notorious pests threatening the food supply. Rodents cause a lot of damage in food processing plants, and they are easily capable of spreading disease. Once in a plant, they can multiply rapidly and create a situation that is very difficult to resolve.

Rodent evidence comes in the form of droppings, urine trails, footprints, damaged food, and gnawed containers. They can live just about anywhere there is harborage, and have been known to burrow in walls or underground. In general, they are survivalists...and they present a daunting challenge in terms of eradication.

Food processors need to rodent-proof their facilities. This is done by sealing all openings/gaps and eliminating harborage, such as unused equipment and machinery, inside and outside of plants. Indoor traps and outdoor poison bait stations are also used as defense mechanisms. If rodents do enter the building, they need to be immediately destroyed to prevent food adulteration.

Insects

These pests might not be as notorious in food plants as rodents, but they are more common. Insects include flies, mosquitoes, cockroaches, and spiders...and they are capable of transmitting disease and contaminating food products.

Insects can be found dead or alive in food...with some even using the food as their homes. They mostly live in non-refrigerated environments, and most prefer processing areas that are slightly warmer than normal room temperature. They typically do not pose the same level of threat as rodents, but they can be difficult to eliminate once they enter processing areas.

Food processors need to insect-proof their facilities. This is done by sealing all openings/gaps and eliminating harborage, such as pooling water, inside and outside of plants. Glue boards and insect-o-cuters are also used as defense mechanisms. If insects do enter the building, they need to controlled or destroyed to prevent food adulteration.

The following is an excerpt from a basic pest control program that might be written for a pasta processing plant:

A. *Housekeeping: All processing areas and equipment will be cleaned daily if used or whenever necessary. All storage areas will be kept clean and uncluttered.*
B. *Structural: All drains will be equipped with screens and/or covers. All potential rodent entrance points, such as cracks and holes, will be repaired immediately.*
C. *Exterior: The premises will be kept clean and uncluttered. lawn, weeds, and brush will be kept trimmed. All areas of harborage will be eliminated.*
D. *A current list of all pesticides in use will be maintained. All pesticides will be EPA approved.*

E. **Rodenticides:** Rodenticides will be placed in bait boxes at designated areas outside the building. The rodenticide bait will be a distinctive blue-green color for identification purposes. Bait boxes will be checked monthly and recorded on the Rodent Control Service Record.
F. **Rodent Stations:** Rodent stations will be placed at designated areas every 30 feet inside the non-production areas of the building. Rodent stations will be checked weekly and recorded on the In-House Rodent Control Service Record.
G. **Electronic Insect Control:** Electronic "Insect-A-Cutors" are placed strategically throughout the plant in non-production areas. The catch pans are large enough to ensure that dead insects will not fall to the floor. The pans will be cleaned bi-monthly, or sooner if necessary, during periods of use.
H. **Sticky Board Insect Control:** Sticky board insect control traps will be placed in production areas. These are changed as needed based on the insect populations seen on the boards.
I. **Detection of Rodent Evidence:** If rodents or evidence of rodents is detected in the plant the following action will be taken:

1. Operations are immediately stopped in the affected area.
2. All packaging materials and containers are examined for rodent damage and discarded if contaminated.
4. Product showing evidence of rodent contamination is condemned, placed in inedible containers, and denatured.
5. All harborage is removed from the area.
6. The entire area and equipment are completely washed and sanitized.
7. A complete survey of the plant and premises is taken to ensure that all points of entry and areas of harborage are eliminated.
8. Production will resume after plant personnel are satisfied that the problem is corrected and the area is cleaned.

Now that you understand many of the internal and external food safety requirements imposed on food processors, let's move into a discussion on a topic that has gained a lot of attention regarding food safety. That topic is allergens.

Allergens

Food allergies occur when people's immune systems have abnormal responses to food. Sensitivity to allergens varies from person to person, but worst case sceneries result in death.

For food safety reasons, food processors should have written programs in place that address the allergens they are using in their products. These programs help make certain that allergens are properly listed on ingredient statements and monitored for misuse and cross-contamination.

The major eight food allergens are soy, wheat, milk, eggs, fish, shellfish, peanuts, and tree nuts. These allergens are described below.

Soy

This is likely the most common allergy. The symptoms of soy reactions are usually mild, but certain cases are more severe. FDA law dictates that soy must be listed in ingredient statements if it is used in food products. However, some processors fail to adhere to this law, and that failure can result in allergic reactions and recalls.

Food or food ingredients containing soy include:

- Miso
- Soya
- Soybean
- Soy fiber
- Soy flour
- Soy milk
- Soy protein
- Soy sauce
- Tempeh
- Textured vegetable protein
- Tofu

Wheat

The bad news about wheat allergies is that they are most common in children. The good news about wheat allergens is that children usually outgrow them before they become adults.

The symptoms of wheat reactions range from mild to severe, and FDA law dictates wheat must be listed on ingredient statements of products containing it. However, some products, such as dextrose made from wheat, do not list wheat…so food processors are not aware that it is present.

Wheat allergies should not be confused with the gluten intolerance associated with individuals suffering from Celiac Disease. Gluten is a combination of proteins found in wheat, rye, oats, barley, spelt, and other similar grains. Wheat allergies typically cause hives, itching, and breathing difficulties, while gluten intolerance results in more severe problems including permanent damage of intestines.

Food or food ingredients containing wheat include:

- Breadcrumbs
- Bulgur
- Cereal extract
- Couscous
- Cracker meal
- Durum
- Einkorn

- Emmer
- Farina
- Flour (various types)
- Hydrolyzed wheat protein
- Matzah
- Pasta
- Seitan
- Semolina
- Spelt
- Triticale
- Wheat bran
- Wheat durum
- Wheat germ
- Wheat gluten
- Wheatgrass
- Wheat malt
- Wheat protein
- Wheat starch

Milk

Similar to wheat allergies, milk allergies are also more common in children who outgrow them later in life. Symptoms range from mild to severe, and FDA law dictates milk must be listed on ingredient statements of products containing it.

Milk allergies should not be confused with lactose intolerance. Lactose intolerant individuals lack the enzyme necessary to digest the sugar lactose. The inability to digest lactose results in extreme intestinal discomfort…unlike the typical hives and itching that result from milk allergies.

Food or food ingredients containing milk include:

- Butter
- Buttermilk
- Candy
- Caramel
- Casein
- Cheese
- Chocolate
- Cottage cheese
- Cream
- Custard
- Evaporated milk
- Ghee
- Half-and-half
- Milk (all types)
- Milk powder
- Milk protein

- Pudding
- Sour cream
- Whey (all forms)
- Whey protein hydrolysate
- Yogurt

Egg

Similar to milk and wheat, egg allergies are also common in children. The whites contain the harmful allergenic proteins, but individuals with allergies need to avoid consuming any part of the egg. Symptoms range from mild to severe, and FDA law dictates egg must be listed on ingredient statements of products containing it.

Food or food ingredients containing egg include:

- Albumen
- Dried egg
- Eggnog
- Egg white
- Egg yolk
- Lysozyme
- Mayonnaise
- Meringue
- Powdered egg
- Ovalbumin
- Surimi

Fish

Fish allergies affect people of all ages, and many individuals do not outgrow them. Symptoms can be very severe, and FDA law dictates fish must be listed on ingredient statements of products containing it.

Food or food ingredients containing fish include:

- Anchovies
- Bass
- Catfish
- Cod
- Flounder
- Grouper
- Haddock
- Hake
- Halibut
- Herring
- Perch
- Pike

- Pollock
- Salmon
- Swordfish
- Sole
- Trout
- Tuna

Shellfish

Fish allergies affect people of all ages, and many individuals do not outgrow them. In fact, some people do not experience their first allergic reaction until well into adulthood. Symptoms can be very severe, and FDA law dictates shellfish must be listed on ingredient statements of products containing it.

Food or food ingredients containing shellfish include:

- Barnacle
- Clams
- Crab
- Crayfish
- Krill
- Lobster
- Mussels
- Oysters
- Prawns
- Scallops
- Scampi
- Shrimp

Peanut

Peanut allergies are fairly common in people of all ages. However, symptoms stand out from other allergies because they can be fatal. Simply touching products containing peanuts can trigger allergic reactions, and people die every year from peanut ingestion. FDA law dictates peanuts must be listed on ingredient statements of products containing them.

Peanuts should not be confused with tree nuts. Peanuts are part of the legume family and grow underground, while tree nuts are true nuts and grow on trees.

Food or food ingredients where peanuts are commonly found include:

- Bread
- Cake
- Candy
- Chocolate
- Coffee Cake
- Croissants

- Donuts
- Fudge
- Ice cream
- Peanuts
- Peanut brittle
- Peanut butter
- Rolls
- Salads

Tree nut

Tree nut allergies occur in adults and children, and people usually do not outgrow them. Symptoms can be severe...even resulting in death in some rare situations.

As noted earlier, tree nuts grow on trees, and they are part of the nut family. They are not part of the legume family that includes peanuts.

Food or food ingredients where tree nuts are commonly found include:

- Almond
- Beechnut
- Brazil nut
- Bread
- Butternut
- Cake
- Candy
- Cashew
- Chestnut
- Chocolate
- Coffee Cake
- Croissants
- Donuts
- Filbert
- Fudge
- Hickory nut
- Ice cream
- Macadamia nut
- Nut butters (cashew butter, pecan butter)
- Nut meal
- Nut milk (cashew milk, almond milk)
- Nut paste (filbert paste, almond paste)
- Pecan
- Pili nut
- Pine nut
- Pistachio
- Praline
- Rolls

- Salads
- Shea nut
- Walnut

People are also allergic to other foods, but these allergies are not quite as common as the eight listed above. These other foods include:

Sesame

Sesame allergies occur in people of all ages, and the number of individuals experiencing effects appears to be increasing. Symptoms can be mild to severe, depending on the sensitivity of the person.

Food or food ingredients where sesame is commonly found include:

- Benne
- Bread
- Coffee cake
- Halvah
- Sesame flour
- Sesame oil
- Sesame paste
- Sesame salt
- Sesame seed
- Sesemolina
- Sim
- Tahini
- Turkish cake

Mustard

Mustard allegories are less common than other allergies, but they are a problem for some people. Canada considers mustard a major allergen, but the United States does not. Symptoms can be mild to severe depending on sensitivity.

Food or food ingredients where mustard is commonly found include:

- Barbeque Sauce
- Curry
- Mayonnaise
- Mustard
- Mustard oil
- Mustard seed
- Pickles
- Pizza
- Processed meats

- Salads
- Salad dressings

Other

Some people also experience allergic reactions to corn and meat. Since corn is used in many different foods, this can be a problem. Along the same lines, meat is a "center of the plate" item that is consumed daily by many people…so it can also present issues.

Sulfites are the last item that needs to be mentioned in this section. They present a sensitivity issue for some people, and allergen type symptoms can result.

Food or food ingredients where sulfites are commonly found include:

- Bakery items
- Beer
- Candy
- Canned vegetables
- Cider
- Condiments
- Dried fruit
- Gravy
- Jellies and jams
- Lemmon Juice
- Maraschino cherries
- Molasses
- Pickled food
- Potassium bisulfite
- Sulfite
- Sulfur dioxide
- Vegetable juice
- Wine

Allergen program

The following is an example of a basic allergen program that might be written for a specialty croissant processing plant:

A. **Allergens consist of the following:**

Milk, soy, fish, peanuts, tree nuts (e.g., almonds, pecans, walnuts), shellfish, eggs, wheat, mustard, sesame, and sulfites

The following allergens may be used in our products:

Soy protein, wheat flour, milk, egg yolks, peanut oil

B. Pallets of ingredients are identified with the specific allergen upon being received.

C. Allergens are stored in designated areas and identified.

D. Copies of formulas for all items are on file electronically.

E. Scaled ingredients list applicable allergens.

F. Ingredient labels follow products throughout processing (work in process) to ensure that allergens are listed on every rack of product.

G. Purchasing has informed all ingredient suppliers that ingredient statements cannot be changed without prior notice.

H. Color-coded or labeled scoops are used for allergens and other ingredients with the potential to cause adverse reactions as follows:

- Blue – Soy
- Marked Blue – Wheat
- Green – Milk
- White – Egg
- Clear - Peanuts

I. Spillage - in the event of allergen spillage the following will be done:

- **Solid Allergen Spillage**

  Details will be recorded in the Allergen Spillage Log. The situation will be risk assessed for potential cross-contamination, and any cross-contaminated product will be put in the trash. The area will be cleaned with dedicated cleaning equipment and damaged product will be put in the trash.

- **Liquid Allergen Spillage**

  Details will be recorded in the Allergen Spillage Log. The situation will be risk assessed for potential cross-contamination, and any cross-contaminated product will be put in the trash. Paper towels will be used to remove the product and put it in the trash. The floor will then be washed.

J. Products containing allergens are physically separated by racks that do not allow cross contamination.

K. Product flow from receiving to shipping is one way to minimize cross contamination.

L. For traceability purposes, ingredient codes used in each batch of product are logged on a checklist.

M. Production lines are cleaned (using wipes or sanitizer) between unlike products. All processing areas are cleaned daily after production is finished.

N. Employees change aprons, sleeves, and gloves when moving from one line to another or working on products containing different allergens.

O. All finished products meet FDA labeling specifications.

P. For traceability and identification purposes, all finished products are coded with a "sell by," "pack date," "use or freeze by," lot number, and/or Julian code.

Q. Allergen testing will be conducted quarterly to verify the program is working. Testing consists of swabbing a food contact line after a product with a known allergen has passed over that line and the line has been cleaned in preparation for the next product. If results show greater than 5 ppm of the known allergen, then the allergen program needs to be re-assessed.

Now you understand the relationship between allergens and food safety. Next, let's look at the action taken when products with food safety concerns inadvertently reach the public. This action is commonly known as a recall.

Recalls

Recalls occur when food products available to the public pose some type of health risk. This risk can occur for a variety of different reasons, but the most common factors are listed below.

Health hazards

This refers to recalls that result from biological, chemical, or physical hazards reaching the public. An example is as follows:

The Stanford Salad Company processes pasta salad that they sell to delicatessens. A deli manager receives a complaint from two different customers that they became ill after eating some of Sanford's product. Both customers ate pasta salad with a lot number of 6315. This is alarming to the deli manager, and he pulls the product from his counter. He promptly notifies Sanford that lot 6315 pasta salad has a problem.

Sanford obtains some of lot 6315 pasta and sends it out to a laboratory for microbial analysis. They find that it is contaminated with Listeria monocytogenes...a potentially deadly bacterium. They also analyze other lots of the same products and find that they are not contaminated with any pathogens.

Based on their findings, Sanford recalls all pasta with a lot number of 6315. This is an entire day of production, and it results in over 2000 pounds of pasta salad being recalled.

This recall resulted from a biological hazard, Listeria monocytogenes, which was in the product when it reached consumers.

Allergens

This refers to recalls that result from products containing allergens that are not listed on the ingredient statements. An example is as follows:

The Holland Bros. Bakery manufactures bread and rolls for hotel chains. They make a sweet roll that contains pecans for hotel brunches, and this product is distributed all over the city of Chicago.

A hotel guest becomes ill after eating one of Holland Bros. sweet rolls. She breaks out with hives and has difficulty breathing. She knows she can eat pecans....but she is allegoric to peanuts. She informs the hotel manager, and the manager calls Robert Holland, president of Holland Bros. Bakery, to tell him what happened.

Robert checks his production records and finds that his employees mixed peanuts in the affected batch of sweet rolls instead of pecans. Robert promptly begins to recall this lot of sweet rolls. Fortunately, all of this lot (22 dozen rolls) went to the same hotel chain, so he is able to get it back to his facility by making a few phone calls.

This recall resulted from an allergen, peanuts, which were in the product when it reached consumers.

Lack of inspection

This is the most interesting reason for a recall, and it is likely the least understood by the general public. USDA processing plants can only produce meat and poultry products when USDA inspectors are on the job. If they process product during hours that USDA inspectors are not working, the product made during that time is subject to a recall if leaves the control of the processing establishment.

Selander Meat International (SMI) produces fresh sausage products for restaurants. They normally work Monday through Friday to complete orders, but they have a machine breakdown and need to produce sausage on Saturday.

SMI schedules production on Saturday, but they forget to let the USDA inspector know that they are working. A week later, the USDA inspector is reviewing records and notices the Saturday production. He asks where this product is located and is told that it has been shipped.

The USDA inspector calls his boss, and she mandates a recall because SMI operated without "the benefit of inspection." They have to contact three different distributors, who get the word out to the restaurants that have purchased the product. Over 8000 pounds of sausage is recalled.

This recall resulted from a lack of inspection in a USDA regulated facility.

Recall program

The following is an excerpt of a basic recall program that might be written for an ice cream processor:

A. **RECALL CLASSIFICATIONS**

1. *Class I. A situation where there is a reasonable probability that use of the product will cause a serious health hazard including death.*
2. *Class II. A situation where there is a remote possibility of adverse health consequences from use of the product.*
3. *Class III. A situation where use of the product is very unlikely to cause adverse health consequences.*

B. **RECALL PROCEDURES**

1. *Health Hazard Evaluation*

   a. *An evaluation of the product being considered for recall will be conducted by plant management by examining:*

      i. *The nature of the defect.*
      ii. *Whether any illness or injuries have occurred from use of the product.*
      iii. *Assessment of the likelihood of occurrence of the hazard.*
      iv. *Assessment of potential consequences of occurrence of the hazard.*

2. *Recall Classification will be assigned based on the health hazard evaluation.*

C. **RECALL STRATEGY**

1. *This strategy will assist in, not dictate, the conduct of a recall. Using the recall classification assigned, the strategy will list:*

   a. *The amount of product being recalled.*
   b. *The extent of information being made available to customers or the public (including notices to the public and customers).*

            c. The action plan to be used for the removal, return, correction, or destruction of the product.

    2. Elements of the strategy will include:

            a. Results of the health hazard evaluation.
            b. Total amount of product involved (based on production records).
            d. Total product distribution (based on invoices containing code dating information).
            e. Action planned by recall (destination of product, FDA notification, public announcement, etc.).
            d. An investigation will occur that determines the cause of the recall.

    3. The Recall Strategy is implemented under the supervision of the Food Safety Director.

    4. Termination of Recall

            a. A recall will be considered concluded when plant management is satisfied that the recall action is completed, proper disposition has been made of the product in violation and no further emergency action is needed.
            b. FDA will be notified of any termination of recall.

D. Mock Recalls

    1. Mock recalls will be performed twice yearly and documented on the Product Recall Form. Documentation will include the date, time started and finished, amount of product produced, and amount of product recovered.
    2. Specifically, each recall will involve one lot of one product that has been processed at our facility. Any product remaining in the shipping freezer along with all customers who have received that product will be identified (based on physical verification and invoices including code dating information) and documented until all pieces or pounds of that product have been accounted for.

Summary

Food safety is paramount for food processors today. Without it, unsafe food reaches consumers, and illness and death can result. When this happens, millions of dollars are spent, company reputations are ruined, and people's lives are destroyed.

This book focuses on food safety for food processors. First, it explores rules and regulations imposed by government agencies, customers, and the processing plants themselves (including GMP, SSOP, HACCP, Food Security, and Pest Control programs). Next, it analyzes the allergens and allergen programs used by food manufacturers. Last, but certainly not least, it examines the types of recalls and recall programs implemented by food processors when unsafe product reaches the public.

Congratulations! You now understand more about food safety...a critical aspect of food processing.

Quality Assurance in Manufacturing
Explaining and Understanding

Louis Bevoc

Published by
NutriNiche System LLC

For information contact:
Info@nutriniche.com

Louis Bevoc books...simple explanations of complex subjects

Introduction 46
    Customer satisfaction 46
    Organizational savings 46

Clarification 46
    Quality assurance 47
    Quality control 47

Implementation 47
    Part A 47
    Part B 49

Advantages 50
    Continuous improvement 50
    Production 50
    Customer satisfaction 51
    Cost savings 51
    Organization 51
    Participation 52

Challenges 52
    Production/quality conflicts 52
    The blame game 52
    Cutbacks 53
    Stress 53
    High expectations 53
    Production training 54

Improving 54
    Draw correlations 54
    Change perception 55
    Allow self-evaluation 55
    Implement training 55
    Provide feedback 57

Future 57
    Increased regulatory intervention 57
    Increased customer intervention 58
    Increased technology 58

Increased globalization of standards	58
Increased importance on cost	59
Increased emphasis on team work	59
Increased ties to safety	59

Summary 60

Introduction

Some people think that quality assurance started in Japan during the 1950s due to poor perception of the products they produced. The Japanese indeed embraced the quality concept, but they were not the first to implement it as part of the ongoing process.

The first organized form of quality assurance took place in the United States during the Second World War. The US government did not want malfunctioning equipment or supplies in the field during the heat of a battle, so they developed procedures to check defects after items were manufactured. This concept stopped defective products from being released for use, thereby preventing many problems for American troops.

After the war, the idea of quality assurance took root with non-military manufacturers, but it was modified to develop procedures for detecting defects before products were finished. Quality checks were still performed on finished items, but procedures were also implemented during the process for preventative measures. This was beneficial for two reasons:

Customer satisfaction

Similar to the military application, defects in products were eliminated before they reached the consumer. This resulted in a higher level of customer satisfaction, fewer complaints, and fewer returns.

Organizational savings

Since checks were ongoing, errors were discovered before the finished product stage. This meant that products did not have to be broken down and reassembled to eliminate defects. In short, the "first loss is the best loss" mentality was implemented so products could be stopped during assembly before additional time and effort were wasted attempting to complete the process.

Today, quality assurance personnel develop procedures for making sure products meet specified requirements. This assures customers that their purchases will adhere to pre-established standards, thereby increasing their confidence that they are dealing with a credible organization.

Virtually every organization employs some type of quality assurance, and many companies have separate departments for the work involved. Employees in these departments seek to improve processes by developing procedures that assure products adhere to specified quality standards. This allows organizations to sell consistent products and remain competitive in markets that demand uniformity.

Clarification

Quality assurance should not be confused with quality control. They have similar functions and are both part of quality management, but they are not the same. The following explains some of their differences:

Quality assurance

This process is used to make sure quality procedures are appropriate and in place for products. It assures the quality of products by establishing standards that prevent defects.

For example, a meat processing plant needs to make sure all hot dogs meet a color requirement. The quality assurance people develop a color chart that can be used as a standard. This chart is implemented in the plant as a mandatory color check on every batch of hot dogs before packaging.

Quality control

This process is used to verify the quality of products. It controls the quality of products using established standards that will detect defects.

Consider the hot dog example in the meat processing plant. Quality control technicians use the color chart developed by quality assurance people to check every batch of product before packaging. If the color does not match, the hot dogs are rejected.

Now that the difference between quality assurance and quality control is understood, it is time to move on to the next section on the implementation of quality assurance programs.

Implementation

Quality assurance programs are critical for manufacturers. They make sure procedures are in place to prevent defects, malfunctioning, and other finished product problems. Manufacturers without quality assurance programs need to implement them, and the following shows the two-part process necessary to accomplish that implementation:

Part A

Below are the six steps necessary to put a quality insurance program in place. They do not complete the process, but they develop it and put it into action.

1. *Define objectives*

    Before a quality assurance program can be implemented, it needs a purpose. In other words, it needs to have defined goals and a concrete purpose. Once the objectives are defined, the organization understands the direction it needs to take, and the implementation process can begin.

    For example, a pet supply manufacturer decides to make a dog leash. They have done the research and found that most leashes break after frequent use. This is a major problem for dog owners, so the pet supply company wants to make a better product.

2. *Define success*

   The objectives are in place, so now the dynamics need to be defined. Which product attributes are the most important? How can the monitoring of those attributes be incorporated into the quality assurance program?

   Durability is the most important attribute of the dog leash for the pet supply manufacturer, so durability must be incorporated into the quality assurance program. This is done by developing procedures designed to measure durability during the manufacturing process.

3. *Define customer base*

   Who is going to use the dog leash? Is it geared for trainers or breeders? Is it meant for small dogs or large dogs?

   The pet supply manufacturer wants their new leash to be geared for large dogs kept as pets by families. They are not targeting trainers or breeders, and their main customer base is determined to be middle-class suburban men and women who walk their dogs in parks.

4. *Define customer needs*

   Durability has already been defined as a need, but other potential customer needs must also be investigated. Is there a color preference? Should the leash look fancy or practical? Is price a concern?

   The pet supply manufacturer determines that their customer base wants dark colors to hide the dirt. They also find that a fancy look is not important, and price is not a major concern.

5. *Define quality procedures*

   After the product and customer base have been defined, it is time to establish procedures for the quality assurance program.

   The pet supply manufacturer decides the leash will be dark blue in color, so they develop a color chart to measure the intensity of the blue. They also decide the leash needs to easily connect to a dog's collar, so they develop a procedure to manually check the connection every hour. Last, they want to use materials that are flexible and durable, so they develop a purchasing specification for the raw material.

6. *Define quality tools*

   Tools are the paperwork, software, instruments, and equipment needed to perform the designated procedures. They are provided to the employees performing quality checks on the product.

The pet supply manufacturer employees need the following tools to perform checks:

- Color chart
- Purchasing specification for raw materials
- Software to compute statistical deviations from specifications
- Tablet (computer) to record data, identify deviations from specifications, and list corrective actions

Part B

Now the program has been put into action. However, this does not complete the implementation process. The program still has to assure quality, so it is time to measure the data and react to the findings. This is done using the following four steps:

1. *Collect data*

    Data must be collected before it has any value. In this step, employees gather information from the procedural checks for subsequent analysis.

    The pet supply manufacturer collects a variety of different data. They obtain the number of leashes that did adhere to color requirements, the frequency of connection failures, and the occurrences where raw materials that did not meet specifications. After this information is gathered, it is used in the next step for analysis.

2. *Analyze data*

    This is where the collected data is analyzed. Findings are used to determine if original objectives are being achieved.

    Quality assurance at the pet supply manufacturer examines statistics and percentages to look for trends of quality related issues. The results are then analyzed and decisions are made regarding the success of the program.

3. *Adjust procedures*

    If the program is deemed successful, then it will continue on in its current capacity. However, if poor quality trends are the result of failures, then changes to the program must be made.

    The pet food supplier finds that the leash connection device is failing at a rate of two percent. Quality assurance determines that two percent is too high for this product, so a minor mechanical adjustment is made, and the frequency of the manual check is increased from every hour to every half-hour. If the failure rate stays the same or increases over the next week, the connection will be redesigned by engineers in the organization.

4. Monitor

If procedures have been adjusted and the quality is considered acceptable, then those procedures must be continuously monitored to assure that quality does not decrease.

The pet food supply company finds the mechanical adjustment of the leash connection device is successful. The failure rate drops to below one-half percent, and this is acceptable. Based on this analysis, quality assurance changes the manual check frequency back to every hour, and they will watch the failure rate closely to assure there is no reoccurrence.

Now you have an understanding of a basic implementation procedure for a quality assurance program. The next section focuses on the reasons that this type of program is beneficial for organizations.

Advantages

There many advantages for organizations that have quality assurance plans in place. Some of these are more important than others, so the focus in this section will be on the most significant benefits. These are as follows:

Continuous improvement

Continuous improvement employs the thinking that everything can be improved. In other words, there is no status quo, and efforts are constantly made to raise the bar. Some of the changes resulting from this process are immediately apparent, while others are not so obvious and take time to transpire. Changes that transpire over time are often the preferred method of continuous improvement because they allow employees time to adjust to workplace modifications.

Of all the advantages, continuous improvement is the easiest to understand because it is the ultimate goal of every quality assurance program. This advantage is apparent after a quality assurance program has been up and running for a while because the goal of always getting better turns into reality. Designated procedures and checks continually search for process and product problems so they can be brought to light, resolved, and prevented from reoccurring. This constant vigilance means organizations continue to progress and manufacture better products.

Production

One might question how production is an advantage of quality assurance programs. After all, quality procedures seem like they would hinder production processes rather than help them. Yes, quality assurance does hinder production, but only for the short term. In the long run, it improves production because problems associated with products are identified and prevented from reoccurring. This stops defects from getting into finished products, causing those products to be reworked or reproduced...at the expense of production.

Customer satisfaction

This is likely the biggest advantage of quality assurance programs. Products are manufactured so they can be sold to customers. If those customers are not happy with the items they purchase, then they return them and/or never buy them again.

Quality assurance verifies products are being manufactured according to specifications. Procedures are designed to identify discrepancies and bring attention to them. Changes are then made to address those discrepancies and prevent them from reoccurring. These changes lead to a happier customer base, increased sales, and fewer headaches for management.

Customer returns and dissatisfaction are huge negatives for organizations. They lower profitability, increase stress and decrease morale. Customers might not always be right, but they are always important...and quality assurance brings that importance to the forefront.

Cost savings

Most manufacturers are looking for cost savings due to the highly competitive markets that they face today...and they find those savings with quality assurance programs. How does this work? It works by measuring how effectively the products are produced. Standards and procedures increase quality and consistency, ultimately leading to better products and higher sales.

Specifically, quality assurance programs:

- Decrease employee mistakes that create waste
- Decrease employee miscommunication that leads to errors
- Decrease reoccurrence of problems that lead to reoccurring costs
- Decrease customer complaints that require resources for response
- Increase employee awareness that prevents mishaps
- Increase employee efficiency that leads to higher productive
- Increase product consistency that results in fewer returns
- Increase customer demand that drives up sales volume

Quality assurance programs cost money for personnel, equipment, supplies, and other resources. However, those resources combine to make better products and reduce misunderstanding by standardizing processes and procedures. This translates to cost savings for manufacturers, and it makes the payback well worth the investment.

Organization

Workplace organization is one of the least obvious benefits of quality assurance. The processes and procedures to control quality also dictate the manner in which production is accomplished. In this respect, they act as behavioral guidelines with step-by-step processes that are followed in the same order every time a product is produced. This prevents the chaos that can result from unstructured environments....and it keeps manufacturers organized.

Organization is a sought after aspect of every manufacturer because it leads to effectiveness and efficiency in the workplace. It keeps employees on task and prevents unnecessary or unproductive activity from occurring. In short, productivity improves as organizations get better, and organizations get better with the implementation of quality assurance programs.

Participation

This refers to employee participation. If employees sense that quality assurance programs are making their organizations more successful, then they buy into the process and begin to make quality a priority. They gain a sense of responsibility and take ownership of their jobs. This change is gradual and might not be readily noticeable, but it does happen.

People who think that employees will not buy into effective quality assurance programs over time are wrong. Successful organizations all over the world have utilized quality programs to achieve goals and objectives, and this would not have been possible without employees working together toward continuous improvement.

As you can see, quality assurance programs produce a variety of benefits. However, these programs are not without problems, and that is why challenges are the focus of the next section.

Challenges

Most good things in organizations have some negatives associated with them, and quality assurance programs are no exception. Despite all the positive aspects, there are some shortcomings. Quality control personnel face challenges that need to be overcome before the programs they implement can become successful.

These challenges include:

Production/quality conflicts

Conflict between production employees and quality personnel is likely the most common drawback of quality assurance programs. This is somewhat expected because both departments have job-related tasks to complete, and those tasks are often opposite to each other.

Quality assurance people implement programs that control the way products are manufactured, and many times this impedes the way production people want to do their jobs. Specific procedures dictate how jobs are performed, and those procedures are not always the easiest or most convenient.

The blame game

It is very easy to place blame for finished product problems on quality assurance people. This is because these problems relate back to issues that occurred during the manufacturing process. Quality assurance personnel are responsible for implementing procedures that prevent these issues from happening, so they are the most logical people to blame.

In reality, problems are always going to occur during manufacturing. People are going to make mistakes even if there are procedures in place to prevent them from doing so because procedures are not 100 percent foolproof. It is not fair to blame quality assurance for problems with finished products, but it does happen and it likely will never completely stop. This is why the "blame game" is a challenge for quality assurance people in manufacturing.

Cutbacks

Quality assurance is a very interesting concept. Many organizational leaders indicate it is one of the most important aspects of manufacturing. However, during tough economic times, it is often one of the first departments where employees are laid off. This is because quality assurance personnel are not essential for the physical assembly of products and are therefore expendable when money is tight.

Manufacturers often depend on consistent products, and that consistency is lost when quality assurance departments are eliminated. One might think that this would indicate the importance of quality assurance personnel regardless of the financial situation. However, this is not typically the case...and it the reason why cutbacks are a challenge for quality assurance.

Stress

Quality assurance programs are capable of causing a lot of stress to people within the department. Decisions need to be made that can cause downtime in production, upset people, and make it seem like quality assurance personnel are the "bad guys" who do not care about the well-being of the organization or the people within it.

Leaders of organizations understand that quality assurance people are not out to inflict harm on the organizations that employ them. In fact, their job is to do the exact opposite. They only stop production to make the manufacturing process better in terms of quality and consistency. However, some people's perceptions of quality assurance personnel are negative...and those perceptions are their reality.

Quality assurance personnel want the best for their organizations, but their decisions can slow or halt productivity. They are well aware of the impact of their actions, and the fact that some people will dislike them. Because of this, some quality assurance personnel cannot handle the stress and end up leaving the department.

High expectations

As noted eagerly, continuous improvement means the bar is constantly being raised in terms of quality and consistency. This is great for organizations, but it can be difficult for employees...and quality assurance personnel are charged with the responsibility of making sure those employees rise with the bar.

Additionally, quality assurance people's wages are not always built into the cost of assembling products. They are tangent to the production process, and this means leadership expects them to perform at high levels to justify their wages.

Production training

Manufacturing typically involves a step-by-step process. That process is repeated the same way time after time to produce a consistent product. Some processes are simple, while others are quite complicated...and more complex processes require effective employee training.

Unfortunately, many production employees do not get the proper training they need to effectively follow the procedures developed by quality assurance personnel. They do not understand their role in the quality process, and they need to be monitored closely for mistakes and deviations. This is challenging for quality assurance personnel because they must act as "babysitters" in production situations. It prevents them from concentrating on continuous improvement because their main focus is on getting employees to adhere to current standards.

You can now see that quality assurance programs have positives and negatives associated with them. Manufacturers that these programs in place need them to perform at the highest levels possible...and that is why improvement is the focus of the next section.

Improving

This section needs to be started with an "absolute must." Quality assurance personnel absolutely must NOT report to production supervisors. If this happens, the purpose and function of the quality assurance department are compromised. That being said, any manufacturer that has quality assurance personnel reporting to production management can immediately improve the program by simply changing the organizational hierarchy.

Even if quality assurance does not report to production management, it can be improved. The following are some ways to this:

Draw correlations

The success of quality assurance programs needs to be gauged to assure that they are effective. This is done by measuring customer satisfaction with surveys. The surveys should ask questions about specific areas that were targeted for improvement by quality assurance. For example, if a cell phone manufacturer has procedures in place to make keyboards more sensitive for texting, then a keyboard ease question should be asked.

Results of the surveys should be analyzed to see if there are any correlations between the quality programs implemented and customer satisfaction. If customer satisfaction is high, then the quality assurance programs are working and do not need to change. However, if customer satisfaction is low, then changes need to be made.

Change perception

Quality assurance personnel are not the enemy. They are there to help the company, and the changes they make help produce better products that lead to higher sales. That being said, the perception of quality assurance personnel and the procedures they implement needs to change.

This is done by:

Supplying information

Like most people, employees do not want to be kept in the dark. They want to know why procedures are in place and who will benefit from them. Skepticism results from a lack of information and quality assurance people are viewed as the reason for it. In short, management needs to inform employees of the reasons why quality assurance personnel do what they do.

Encouraging input

Sometimes the best way to get information about specific jobs is to ask the people performing those jobs. They know what needs to be done and have often figured out the best way to do it. They might need to change their ways after they give their input, but they will accept the change more readily because they will feel like they were part of the decision-making process.

Allow self-evaluation

This is probably the most overlooked method of improvement because it requires an analysis of self rather than others. It is relatively easy for employees to point out the shortcomings of their coworkers, but it is usually much more difficult to pinpoint their own faults. Most employees prefer to point out the positive aspects of their job performance rather than those that are not so positive.

Self-evaluation is another form of employee involvement, but it differs because it asks employees to evaluate their own work in terms of quality. They are given the opportunity to look at the part of the manufacturing process that they control and make suggestions for change. The changes they suggest might be small, but they indicate employees' commitment to the continuous improvement of their organizations.

In short, self-evaluation lets employees feel like they are part of the solution instead of being part of the problem.

Implement training

Proper training prevents problems from occurring. When employees are trained to follow quality assurance procedures, they make fewer mistakes, and production lines run more efficiently. This means products can be produced that meet quality, consistency, and cost requirements.

The following are positives that result from employee training in terms of improving quality assurance:

Increased skills

Organizations want their workers to do their jobs more efficiently and effectively, and this requires up-to-date knowledge and understanding of the tasks they perform. That knowledge and understanding are best obtained using some form of employee training.

The most important part about increased employee skills is the fact that they benefit employees and the organization. Workers benefit by becoming more knowledgeable and valuable in their chosen profession, and organizations benefit by having more competent employees to help meet quality goals and objectives.

Increased motivation

Motivation is important in any workplace because it drives employees to perform at optimum levels. Without motivation, workers lack the desire to complete job-related tasks...and this prevents organizations from reaching their potential.

Training allows employees to learn new concepts and better understand the requirements of their jobs. This enables them to work with limited supervision, and the resulting autonomy increases their motivation to make products that meet quality standards.

Increased job satisfaction

Job satisfaction has been defined in many different ways by a variety of sources. For simplicity purposes, this book views it as employees' like or dislike of their jobs.

Training leads to workers liking their jobs because it provides information that helps them complete assigned tasks. This allows them to experience success...and that success increases their desire to produce quality products.

Increased collaboration

Many employees like to share newly acquired knowledge about their jobs. After all, this knowledge has the greatest value in the workplace because other people are working toward achieving the same goals.

Training provides employees with new knowledge, and that knowledge is shared through collaboration with coworkers. This collaboration encourages workers to think differently due to the diversity of the people involved, and the resulting ideas are beneficial for the overall quality of the organization.

Decreased absenteeism and turnover

Training can be a double-edged sword in terms of turnover. It provides knowledge, and that knowledge can be used to find a better job at another organization. However, this is typically not the case because training inspires loyalty in employees....and that loyalty keeps them working for their current employers. That loyalty also inspires them to emphasize quality in their jobs because they identify with their organizations and the products they produce.

Provide feedback

This suggestion is straightforward and simple. Feedback is essential for the improvement of any quality assurance program because employees cannot change if they do not know that they are doing something wrong. They need specific information to accomplish the goal of continual improvement, and that information needs to come from quality assurance personnel.

Employees also like to know when they are doing things right. This makes them feel good about their work and encourages them to continue on the same path. It also motivates workers to take ownership of the jobs they perform. When this happens, they need minimal supervision because they know what needs to be done.

In short, feedback is essential for making employees aware of how they are doing in terms of upholding quality standards.

Future

Due to ever-increasing customer demands, quality assurance personnel will always be necessary in workplaces. In fact, the functions of quality departments will likely grow as organizations move into the future. That growth, however, will come with changes...so expect the following:

Increased regulatory intervention

A major role of democratic governments is to protect the people that they serve. They work for and are paid by the people of the countries they regulate, and their capacity as overseers continues to grow.

Government officials have their hands in many different aspects of organizational operations, and this shows no signs of tapering off in the future. The United States government, for example, continues to grow in size and increase spending. This allows its employees to expand their roles as overseers of organizations...and quality assurance will fall under their jurisdiction.

Increased customer intervention

Customers want to have a say in the products manufactured for them by their suppliers, especially if those products are private labeled. Two major ways they are doing this include:

> *Requirements* (programs, policies, procedures)
>
>> Customers send specific requirements out to the manufacturers of their products. These requirements can dictate processes, specify dimensions, mandate testing, or instruct suppliers to do just about anything else that relates to the quality of the products. If manufacturers refuse to implement these requirements, then they risk losing the business.
>
> *Audits*
>
>> Quality assurance personnel check the actions of production personnel, but who checks the actions of quality assurance personnel? The answer is typically nobody outside of those in top leadership positions...but that is changing, and it will change even more in the future.
>>
>> Customers will conduct their own audits or contract them out to professional organizations. These audits will assure that specified quality standards are being upheld in addition to the status quo standards that are present in every type of manufacturing.

Understandably, customers want some control over the products manufactured for them. The extent of that control is debatable, but the fact remains that it is not going to disappear...now or in the future.

Increased technology

Based on what has happened over the past few decades, it is understandable that technology will play a larger role in the quality assurance of manufacturers. This technology will come in the form of software, hardware, and equipment. For example, software will be needed for statistical analysis, hardware will be essential for portable hand-held devices, and equipment will be required for robotics.

Software, hardware, and equipment will become even more important as global competition between manufacturers increases. Remote access to all aspects of quality assurance will be required...and that requirement will be met with the advent of new technology.

Increased globalization of standards

Organizations are competing in a world market more than they ever have in the past, and this will not slow down in the future. This is great, but it will have some drawbacks. Many countries have their own standards in terms of quality, and this will need to change if they want to work with each other. There will need to be some type of globalization of quality standards. The exact nature of that globalization is yet to be determined, but it will happen...so expect it!

There is no doubt that standards will change as organizations become global, but the goal for continuous improvement will remain the same. There will always be searches for better standards than those being used. Based on this, it also makes sense that the monitoring of global standards will intensify in the future.

Increased importance on cost

Like it or not, cost is a major concern of manufacturers, and this will not change in the future. This will be bad for quality assurance personnel because their expense is often considered unnecessary for the assembly of products....so they will, therefore, be expendable. Unfortunately, some leaders will never get over the thinking that quality takes a back seat to manufacturing.

However, there is also a positive side to the importance of cost. When quality assurance departments do what they are designed to do, they actually save organizations money by reducing manufacturing errors and customer complaints (see *Cost savings* in the *Advantages* section for details). In other words, quality assurance departments provide a good return on the investment. Therefore, the cost of quality assurance in the future will not be a negative factor...as long the programs function effectively.

Increased emphasis on teamwork

One area of quality assurance that will improve in the future is teamwork. Quality assurance personnel do not always get along with manufacturing employees. Workers in these two departments tend to have different immediate priorities even though their long-term goals are the same. This cannot happen in organizations that have goals of growth and prosperity...and the future will bring about preventative change.

The reduction of conflict between quality assurance and production workers will present some challenges, but it will happen...and the first major step forward will involve empathy training. Employees will learn to understand the difficulties of each other's jobs by "putting themselves in their coworker's shoes." Once they begin to understand each other's roles, the door to teamwork will open wide.

Increased ties to safety

Quality is often tied to safety because regulated processes and procedures prevent employees from making mistakes that could be injurious or deadly. Workers are forced to stay on a proven path because there are consequences for not doing so.

A natural progression for quality assurance is to move into the area of safety management. They understand how to write programs for continual improvement, and the same thinking can be applied to safety in manufacturing plants. This is not necessarily the way it is now, but quality assurance will be involved with safety in the future.

Summary

Quality assurance is important for any manufacturing organization. It ensures that the products produced meet quality and consistency standards so customers will be satisfied. It is a proactive process that benefits organizations in many ways.

This book focuses on the quality assurance of products. It describes the topic, discusses its implementation, talks about the advantages and challenges involved, notes methods of improvement, and envisions it in the future. The text is educational and informational, and it is written for easy reader understanding at any level.

Congratulations! You now understand more about quality assurance...an important aspect of any manufacturing organization.

Research and Development in Organizations

An Introduction to Product-Based R&D

Louis Bevoc

Published by
NutriNiche System LLC

For information contact:
Info@nutriniche.com

Louis Bevoc books...simple explanations of complex subjects

Introduction 63
Importance 63
Responsibilities 65
  Researching market trends 65
  Researching new products 65
  Developing new products 66
  Shortening market time 66
  Assessing current products 66
  Maintaining product quality 66
Advantages 67
  Opportunity 67
  Strategy 67
  Uniqueness 67
  Profitability 67
  Image 68
  Cost management 68
  Tax breaks 69
Disadvantages 69
  Uncertainty 69
  Change 69
  Money 70
Improving 70
  Universal standards 70
  Academia and industry collaboration 70
  Better communication 71
Future 71
  Spending 71
  Investment 71
  Global focus 72
Summary 72

Introduction

Organizations that want to grow and prosper need new products and services. Research and Development (also known as R&D) is utilized by organizations to obtain those new products and services. The work of R&D personnel helps companies gain a competitive edge. This is important for every organization...especially those that are heavily impacted by technology.

Rewards for research and development can be very high, but there is also a large potential for failure. In fact, the majority of R&D projects fail long before they make it to the market. Organizations need successful projects to recoup losses on the ones that failed. In other words, there is a lot of risk involved with R&D; and this risk makes it imperative for R&D departments to be well organized and managed.

Much of the R&D done by businesses is conducted in academia. In fact, some companies contract all or most of their R&D out to academic institutions. This is advantageous because many colleges and universities have the necessary personnel, equipment, and laboratories to do the job properly. Academic R&D work is great in terms of efficiency, but the downside is that contracting companies do not learn anything from work being conducted, and they become dependent on academia for new product development. Additionally, companies that rely on academia are not the sole owners of the new products or technology that is developed, so they cannot control it from being used by other organizations.

This book is concerned with the product-based R&D work that takes place in non-academic institutions. More specifically, it examines R&D in organizations that manufacture products.

It is important to note that research and development is not the same as engineering. Some people ask why R&D is needed in manufacturing when engineers essentially do the same work. The answer is because they do not do the same work. Creativity is needed for both jobs, but engineers are an extension of R&D. R&D people develop prototype products for testing in production, and engineers convert those prototypes into items that can be manufactured in volume and sold to customers as finished products.

For this book, research and development is defined as:

> *The creation of new products or improvement of existing products in manufacturing environments*

Now that you understand the scope of this book, let' move on to a discussion on the importance of research and development.

Importance

Innovation drives growth and prosperity, and research and development drives innovation. Astute leaders of manufacturing organizations realize the importance of innovation and they react by funding R&D projects. They realize that research and development is an investment in the future, and it is capable of transforming entire industries.

Good examples of the importance of research and development are automotive manufacturers. They are constantly on the cutting edge of technology, and they do whatever is necessary to compete in today's global marketplace. They have many people working on different vehicles that might or might not be put into production. However, the expense is justified because without innovation....automobile companies cannot compete. New automotive concepts are constantly coming into the market, and the companies that fail to produce novel ideas simply will not survive.

Other examples include food manufacturers. These companies are continually coming up with new food items for their markets. Their R&D departments develop different flavors, sizes, colors, smells, and appearances of food to entice consumers to make purchases. In the food manufacturing business, there truly is a "flavor of the month" that loses its appeal in a relatively short period of time. R&D people are employed to make sure new consumer interest will be consistently generated.

Manufacturers choose to invest in research and development because they understand its importance. They realize they will gain market share and a wealth of knowledge that can be used for growth and prosperity. They understand that the payback is worth the investment because R&D is needed to meet sales expectations.

Some people believe research and development only applies to large manufacturers who compete internationally. After all, these companies have the money to invest in new projects, and they can hire personnel with R&D education and experience. Indeed, large companies are typically financially strong, but small companies also need R&D. Small manufacturers need new products to put on the market...regardless of the size of that market.

Small manufactures have some advantages when it comes to research and development. For example, many of them have management personnel that have "grown up in the business." These individuals have worked a variety of different jobs in their organizations, and they take a hands-on approach to running their businesses. R&D is a natural extension of their job skills, and they are able to create new products due to their understanding of the markets where they compete. In fact, these individuals are sometimes the best choice for R&D regardless of other people's education or experience.

Research and development can be thought of as the major building block of innovation. In fact, most innovation is a direct result of the work of R&D...and this will likely never change. In this sense, R&D is a catalyst for the innovation necessary for gaining a competitive edge. This is a major reason why R&D is important, and it is also a major reason why it is an investment rather than an expense.

Research and development personnel often view problems as opportunities rather than obstacles. For example, household flies are thought of by most people as unwanted pests. They are relatively filthy and quite capable of spreading disease. However, R&D people viewed them as a business opportunity...and that is why they created fly swatters, fly strips, fly baits, and similar fly eradication devices that can are now manufactured in large volumes.

The discussion in this section would not be complete without mentioning the importance of research and development to engineering. As noted earlier, engineers are an extension of R&D. R&D people develop prototypes, and engineers make prototypes production-ready. That being said, organizations that are thought of as world-class in engineering owe much of that status to R&D....and it is another reason why R&D is important. This is the way it was in the past, the way it is now, and it is the way it will be in the future.

Now that you understand some reasons why research and development is important, let's move on to a discussion on the job responsibilities of R&D personnel.

Responsibilities

Two obvious responsibilities of manufacturing R&D personnel are to "research" and "develop" new products. First, they research various aspects of a proposed product to assure that it is worth being developed. Then they develop a prototype of the product using specifications established by management, customers, and regulatory agencies. The end goal is to get the product ready so it can be tested in production.

The above paragraph simplifies the responsibilities of research and development professionals. However, it is not all-encompassing because R&D personnel have many other job functions. For example, they get involved with sales, marketing, production, and quality employees to work on projects and come up with new ideas. They also collaborate with these individuals to uncover product trends that are of value to their organizations.

Managers who oversee the work of research and development people need to understand that a great deal of time and effort are invested in a new product before it reaches the production floor. Specifications, costs, timelines, regulatory requirements, and other aspects of the proposed product must be clearly understood before that product begins to be developed. If there is no demand in the market for the proposed product, then developing it is an unnecessary expense and a waste of time. If the proposed product is considered a viable item that people will purchase, then the next phase of work begins.

The best way to more completely understand the responsibilities of product-based research and development personnel is to list their major job functions. Essentially, these individuals are responsible for:

Researching market trends

Market research for manufacturers involves analyzing general trends of products that are selling in the marketplace. Questions are asked to understand what consumers are buying now and what they might be buying in the future. Which categories are growing? Which categories are declining? Which categories have potential? Which categories should be abandoned? Answers to these questions are used to make decisions about new products that will be developed by R&D personnel. Market research is an important responsibility of R&D personnel because new products require a significant amount of time and effort...and the cost of failure can be very high.

Researching new products

This involves researching specific products that competitors are selling. When a product sells well, it is examined to determine why it is attractive to consumers. Often this involves purchasing the product, taking notes on its appearance, checking its performance, and disassembling it to get a better idea of how it works. This type of research provides direction for developing a competitive product...and it is a direct responsibility of R&D personnel.

Developing new products

Once market trends have been analyzed and a competitive product has been selected, it is time to develop a prototype. Research and development personnel are charged with this responsibility, and it is typically an area where they excel. They have the expertise necessary to create the prototype and deliver it to engineers for testing. In short, research paves the road to development, and development turns concepts into reality.

Shortening market time

Sometimes research and development employees are thought of as roadblocks because they have the final say on whether or not prototypes are ready to be tested in production. It is true that they hold prototypes for certain periods of time, but this holding process is necessary to assure those prototypes are ready for testing in production. R&D efforts eliminate the potential for many different mistakes, thereby preventing "back to the drawing board" situations from transpiring. In this regard, R&D personnel actually shorten the time from product conception to market by applying their expertise and knowledge to make sure prototypes function as intended.

Assessing current products

Another responsibility of research and development personnel involves assessing products that are currently being manufactured and sold. In this capacity, they ensure that these products are still functional and performing as expected. Changes or upgrades to these products might be necessary to make them more effective or efficient in their designated capacities. If R&D personnel believe that a product cannot be improved and or is no longer valuable, then they might choose to discontinue it.

Maintaining product quality

This might be the least common responsibility of R&D personnel, but it does occur in some manufacturers. It expands upon the assessment of current products by performing quality checks on those products after they are running in production. One might question why these checks are done by research and development personnel rather than quality people. The answer is because R&D people are more familiar with product specifications. After all, they have done the research and developed the prototypes for those products. If R&D personnel do not perform the actual checks, they might play a support role for quality assurance people by collaborating with them on quality maintenance.

As you can see, research and development personnel have product responsibilities from conception to implementation and beyond. Based on these responsibilities, it is rather obvious that their work benefits manufacturers as they move into new product ventures. Next, let's examine some specific advantages that R&D personnel provide.

Advantages

The benefits of research and development expand well beyond the laboratories where prototypes are developed. They provide avenues for growth and prosperity, thereby helping organizations successfully move into the future. Manufacturing leaders need to understand the value of R&D by supporting it with the necessary funding and resources. If allowed to do what it is supposed to do, R&D has a very positive impact on organizations.

Specific advantages of research and development are listed below.

Opportunity

Without a doubt, research and development work leads to opportunistic situations. Often this is because R&D personnel are in the right place at the right time, but it also is a result of the earnest effort put forth by these individuals. For example, they might be researching one product, when they discover a trend with another. Another example is getting an idea for a new product based on something else being made by the competition. One last example is an accidental discovery that takes place during the design of a prototype. Regardless of the way opportunities present themselves during the R&D process; their occurrence is advantageous for manufacturing organizations.

Strategy

Research and development helps organizations plan their actions in terms of sales, advertising, and marketing. Sales are grown when research and development identifies trends and specific products that are doing well. This leads to those products being manufactured and sold to the same customer base to gain market share. Marketing professionals rely on R&D to provide novel product designs or features that can be used to attract new customers. Last, but certainly not least, advertising departments create television, radio, and print advertisements based on products developed by R&D personnel. These ads reach hundreds, thousands, or millions of people who previously did not know that these products existed. Strategy helps manufacturers become more competitive, and R&D helps formulate strategy.

Uniqueness

If research and development personnel create a product that stands out from the competition, then they have created a unique product. If that product is very unique, then it can be protected with a patent. Patents prevent copycats from making the same product, and they create a somewhat monopolistic selling environment for a designated amount of time. This sales environment results in more sales, higher profitability, and a healthier organization. R&D personnel strive to created unique products, and those products can be very advantageous for manufacturers.

Profitability

Profitability is critical for virtually every manufacturer, and it only occurs after products start selling consistently. Good R&D leads to consistent selling because products are researched and developed by people who understand their jobs and their industry. When products firmly establish themselves in markets, they have the potential to sell consistently for years...and this leads to long-term profits. In short, R&D leads to profitability due to the work done with products long before they are introduced to the market.

Image

If people have a perception of an organization, then they have established an image. Image is important because it paints a picture of an organization as a whole. Positive image establishes trust with customers and the public, while a negative image has the opposite effect. Manufacturing R&D helps build positive images through new product innovation that drives customer satisfaction.

The following shows how different people are affected by the image of manufacturers:

Employees

Potential employees are attracted to manufacturers with a positive image. They like the thought of working for companies that they think highly of and respect. In fact, some people will even accept a lower wage to work for these organizations rather than working for a company that they view negatively.

Current employees often choose to remain working for organizations that they view positively. They find job satisfaction because they identify with their companies, and this prevents them from looking elsewhere for employment.

Investors

Inventors are enticed by organizations with positive images because it helps them believe that they will receive a return on their investments. This same thinking applies to stockholders who choose to invest in companies that they view in a positive light.

Customers

Reputation is driven by image, and people want to purchase products from organizations they deem reputable. Their loyalty is indicated by the fact that they will pay a higher price for a product from a company they respect even though the same product can be bought cheaper from another organization. Unfortunately, manufacturers with negative images can find it hard to make people think differently...and this negatively affects their bottom lines.

Cost management

Like it or not, cost affects virtually every business decision. It might not be at the top of the list, but it has to get some consideration because most manufacturers are driven by the bottom line. Cost is always a consideration for research and development decisions because R&D is an expense that involves risk with no guarantee of success. However, companies with good R&D departments actually control costs by developing new products as effectively as possible. Personnel from other areas, such as manufacturing or marketing, might know what they need to achieve...but they do not always know how to go about it in the most cost-efficient manner. In the end, they spend more time and money working on new projects than R&D departments.

Tax breaks

The United States government allows companies to use certain percentages of their research and development spending as tax deductions. This book is not designed to get into specific details of those deductions, but the point is that they benefit the manufactures that take them. In this regard, some of the money spent on R&D can be recouped, and this makes the development of new products even more attractive.

Now you understand some of the advantages associated with product-based research and development. However, as might be expected, there are also some negatives associated with manufacturing R&D...and that is why the next section explores disadvantages.

Disadvantages

Effective research and development provides many different benefits to manufactures. It helps them compete, provides them with unique market presence, enhances their reputations, and even helps their bottom lines. However, R&D also has some challenges associated with it. In fact, some manufacturers choose not to invest in it due to the following disadvantages:

Uncertainty

This might be the biggest disadvantage of research and development. Quite simply, it is never known if a new product is going to be successful. It might get out in the market and be successful, but it also might be a total flop. This risk is taken anytime R&D is conducted, and some manufacturers are not willing to accept the potential consequences.

Another aspect of uncertainty involves miscommunication. If R&D personnel do not get a clear picture of what needs to be done, then they might create something that does not work. For example, an R&D department in Arizona might be working on a new electrical component that needs to function properly for at least five years. However, they are not aware that this component has to function in a very humid area of Florida that often reaches temperatures over 100F. This environment will have a huge impact on the electrical component, and it will likely cause it to fail. In short, miscommunication can create a doomed product before it has a chance to enter the market.

Change

Research and development is not a fast process, and this will likely never change. Unfortunately, changes can occur during long periods of time…and those changes can cause the work of R&D personnel to become virtually useless. Customers might decide that they no longer want a product, specifications might be altered, the market might no longer be viable, or a better item might have been introduced. Regardless of what happens, changes that occur over time can cause products to become unwanted or unneeded. This disadvantage is not the fault of R&D personnel, but it can and does occur.

Money

How can money be a disadvantage of R&D if profitability and cost management are both advantages? The answer is because some organizations choose to view it this way…and sometimes with good reason. Without a doubt, there is an upfront cost for research and development. If that cost is not recouped, then it is a loss. Some manufactures simply do not want to set aside money for something that may or may not work for the better of the organization. They choose to limit R&D or conduct it internally with existing management. There is a cost to using internal management for R&D, but not nearly as much as investing in an entire department. However, manufacturers must realize that their potential for large returns on new products diminishes when R&D is limited…and it can result in them becoming less competitive.

Now you understand some of the advantages and disadvantages involved with research and development. Organizations need to weigh the pros and cons before investing in R&D, and this is often a big decision. Money and time are risked if companies choose to conduct R&D, but the ability to compete is risked if they choose to do nothing. This being said, there must be ways to improve R&D…and that is why improvement is the focus of the next section.

Improving

Research and development needs to get better for it to be embraced by manufacturing leaders who are undecided about its worth to their organizations. Some ways to make it better are as follows:

Universal standards

This might be the most overlooked method of improving research and development even though it should be rather obvious. **Universal standards need to provide a reference point for all organizations that conduct product-based R&D. These standards eliminate some of the guesswork in the R&D process, thereby saving time and money that is often spent trying to establish some type of starting point. For example, a food manufacturer trying to make a honey-based salad dressing should have a Food and Drug Administration (FDA) requirement for the minimum amount of honey that must be in the product. This requirement gives a baseline for where to begin developing the product, and it evens the playing field with other food manufacturers who might otherwise choose to use far less of the expensive ingredient.**

Academia and industry collaboration

There must be a stronger bridge built between academia and industry so they can work together on product-based research and development. This collaboration should take place in educational laboratories and organizational settings with the objective being better R&D. Education is the key to developing new ways to become competitive, and organizations that participate in research are on the cutting edge of new ideas and technology. In short, theory and practical application fuel each other in the ever-changing global marketplace...and the strengthening of this relationship is necessary for improving R&D.

Better communication

As noted in the disadvantages section, miscommunication causes big problems for research and development. Fortunately, business leaders and R&D professionals are aware of this problem, but they need to work together to open the lines of communication on a more regular basis. This means decisions cannot be made without consulting everyone involved. There needs to be a plan in place that designates what type of communication will take place at each stage of the process. In terms of R&D, companies that fail to plan are essentially planning to fail.

Better communication also requires feedback after a product has been introduced to the market. Was the product successful? If not, what caused it to fail? The information gathered from constructive feedback helps improve future products by preventing mistakes from being repeated and providing a greater understanding of customer needs. Feedback is valuable, but not enough of it is given in many cases.

Now you have some suggestions for improving research and development as it moves forward. This leads us to the next section that discusses the future of R&D.

Future

This section looks at the future of research and development. Not surprisingly, R&D is going to be around as long as manufacturers compete with each other. They need to develop new products to keep or gain market share, and this can only be done with R&D. That being said, the following specific aspects of R&D will change in the future:

Spending

Manufacturers will become more engrossed in research and development. Leaders will realize the value of R&D and the fact that it cannot be ignored if they want their organizations to grow and prosper. This means spending will increase for R&D projects. That spending will be viewed as an investment rather than a risk even though success is not guaranteed. In this regard, leaders of organizations will change their mindsets about product-based research and development. They will put money aside to make sure projects are properly completed and R&D personnel are never thought of as expendable employees.

Investment

As noted above, spending refers to the money spent internally by manufacturers. However, external funding will also increase in the form of investment. Outside investors will fund research and development projects because they will be more cognizant of the importance of those projects. Without R&D, manufacturers will not grow...and growth is necessary for return on investment.

Along the same lines, people will want to buy stock of manufacturers that are dedicated to research and development. They will understand that R&D fuels growth and growth increases the value of their stock. Stock purchases will create win-win situations for organizations and stockholders because the money obtained will be used to create new products that keep companies healthy and stockholders happy.

Global focus

The focus of product-based research and development will become more worldwide as companies compete in an ever-increasing global market. The research aspect of R&D will consider different customs and cultures when deciding which new products need to be developed. Additionally, technology will make it easier than it ever was in the past to transport products to any destination, and manufactures will take advantage of that technology. In short, the face of R&D will change as the local, regional, and national focus takes a backseat to global demands.

Summary

Product-based research and development is a valuable process that is used by manufacturers all over the world. It helps them remain competitive in ever-changing markets, but that competitiveness comes with the risk of failure. However, based on the need to compete, R&D is necessary for the survival of many companies...and this will likely continue for a long time.

This book focuses on product-based research and development in organizations...primarily manufacturers. It examines the responsibilities of R&D personnel, analyzes the advantages and disadvantages of R&D departments, suggests methods for improving R&D, and assesses the general future of the concept. The text is informational and educational, and it is written for easy reader understanding at all levels.

Congratulations! You now understand more about product-based research and development...a competitive must for manufacturers all over the globe.

Benchmarking in Organizations
Understanding its Importance

Louis Bevoc

Published by
NutriNiche System LLC

For information contact:
Info@nutriniche.com

Louis Bevoc books...simple explanations of complex subjects

Introduction — 75
Example — 75
Types — 76
Methodology — 77
Identify subject — 78
Identify comparative sources — 78
Collect data — 78
Determine differences — 79
Establish goals — 79
Develop plan — 80
Implement plan — 80
Adjust plan — 80
Monitor progress — 80
Inhibiting factors — 82
Resources — 82
Management commitment — 83
Communication — 83
Resistance to change — 84
Benefits — 84
Lower costs — 84
Higher quality — 84
Increased sales — 85
Reduced uncertainty — 85
Enhanced decision-making — 85
Better innovation and creativity — 85
Improving — 85
Plan — 85
Minimize resistance — 86
Validate data — 87
Clarify results — 87
Implement findings — 87
Monitor progress — 87
Summary — 88

Introduction

The term "benchmark" has been around for hundreds of years. Originally, it applied to an actual bench. Shoemakers determined people's shoe sizes by putting their feet on a bench and measuring the length of them with a mark on that bench. This procedure faded away as shoes started to be manufactured for the masses, but the terminology remained.

Surveyors are likely the first people to use benchmarking as a standard. They identified stationary points in geographical areas and measured distances of everything else from those points. This application is not quite the same as that found in organizations today, but the concept grew roots with map building pioneers and gradually changed to its current status.

A benchmark is a standard that organizations strive to reach. It is used to raise the bar for current practices with the ultimate goal of continuous improvement. When properly utilized, benchmarking is an excellent tool for increasing performance and productivity. This helps organizations grow and prosper as they compete in markets that are constantly undergoing change.

Organizations that use benchmarks are searching for best practices. They compare their process and procedures to leading practices in their industry and attempt to raise their own standards. Essentially, the benchmark they have chosen provides them with a snapshot of where they are and where they want to be. This process is never-ending because practices need to be constantly re-evaluated to monitor position and progress...and that is why there is a goal of continuous improvement.

Leaders use benchmarking to make strategic decisions. They are able to measure the critical functions of the workplace and make adjustments. Those adjustments are then monitored to make sure they are working to better the organization as a whole.

When properly executed, benchmarking is a great driver for organizational change. It exposes weaknesses and areas that require improvement using data that was collected and analyzed under a pre-designated plan of action. The results of benchmarking often make people uncomfortable, but sometimes individuals need to leave their comfort zones to better themselves and their organizations.

Example

It might be easiest to envision benchmarking in action by looking at an example that many people, especially those who invest money in the stock market, are familiar with and understand. That example is a mutual fund containing stocks and bonds.

Benchmarks are commonly used as standards by investment companies to measure the success of their own funds and make adjustments to their financial offerings. In short, they choose mutual funds with similar goals and objectives to make comparisons and changes.

It is important to note that the comparison mutual fund must be similar. For example, a conservative fund should not be compared to an aggressive fund because stock market volatility will have a much bigger impact on the aggressive fund. This would be similar to comparing apples and oranges, and conclusions would, therefore, be inaccurate.

It is also critical to understand the reason for the benchmark. In other words, why was this benchmark mutual fund chosen and what is the objective? Is the benchmark fund being mirrored in terms of stock or bond selection? Is the goal to equal the benchmark fund or surpass it? These questions are important because risk-related decisions will be made based on those objectives...and the end result could be financially devastating.

Once the benchmark mutual fund has been chosen and the data has been collected, an analysis is made that determines differences and makes recommendations for change. These recommendations are then implemented to improve the performance of the investment company's fund.

Types

Organizations often differ in the types of benchmarking that they conduct. For example, some companies want to compare groups or departments within their own workplace, while others want to compare groups or departments to those in other workplaces.

Many different factors can be combined to establish specific types. These factors can be homogenous, such as comparing an accounting department to another accounting department. They can also be heterogeneous, such as comparing the goal accomplishment of an accounting department to that of the shipping department.

Homogeneous and heterogeneous factors can be simplified by breaking them into two basic categories known as internal and external. Below are some examples of combinations of factors and categories that create different types of benchmarking.

Homogeneous-Internal

This involves making comparisons of similar groups in the same organization. An example is a bakery with several manufacturing plants. The cake plant wants to improve productivity, so the top-performing cake plant in the organization is used as a benchmark.

Heterogeneous-Internal

This involves making comparisons of dissimilar groups in the same organization. Think about the bakery example. Their top-performing overall plant, a cookie manufacturer, is used as a benchmark to improve the productivity of the cake plant.

Homogeneous-External

This involves making comparisons of similar groups in different organizations. Think about the bakery example. The cake plant wants to improve productivity, so a competitor cake plant that is a top performer in cake manufacturing is used as a benchmark.

Heterogeneous-External

This involves making comparisons of dissimilar groups in different organizations. Think about the bakery example. The cake plant wants to improve productivity, so a competitor pie plant that is a top performer in the bakery industry is used as a benchmark.

Regardless of whether the benchmarking is internal, external, homogeneous, or heterogeneous, it has to be conducted by knowledgeable personnel. This leads to another question. Should benchmarking be conducted by organizations themselves or outside consultants? This is a difficult question to answer because there are advantages and disadvantages to each.

These advantages and disadvantages are as follows:

Organizations doing it themselves

- They can pinpoint their own needs better than outside consultants. They know what they want and what they are looking for in terms of improvement. Some outside consultants take a generic approach to benchmarking simply because they do not have a complete understanding of organizational needs.
- They are less expensive than outside consultants.
- They are concerned about improvement more than outside consultants because their livelihood and reputation are at stake.

External consultants

- They are more objective than organizations doing it themselves. This is good because the organization receives a legitimate analysis from a non-bias firm.
- They are more experienced than organizations doing it by themselves. Since this is what they do as a company, they usually do it well.
- They are considered more legitimate than organizations doing it by themselves because they are professionals. This works well for customers or clients who are looking at purchasing goods or services from the organization undergoing benchmarking.

Now that you understand the meaning of benchmarking and some basic types of this phenomenon, let's move to the next section on a specific benchmarking procedure.

Methodology

There is no universal or "one size fits all" benchmarking procedure. It's not like the National Football League where one set of rules applies for all teams. In fact, as benchmarking becomes more and more popular, a variety of different methodologies have surfaced.

For simplification purposes, this book will focus on some of the most common steps in benchmarking methodologies developed by Motorola and Xerox. The steps consist of the following:

1. Identify subject

This refers to the subject that has been selected for benchmarking. Organizations need to decide what needs to be benchmarked so that specific areas can be compared against another source for improvement.

Subject identification is not always an easy process because organizations often have difficulty defining their weak areas. This is due to "tunnel vision" that results from working in organizations for extended periods of time. Problems might not seem like problems because they have been dealt with for so long. They are overlooked because this is what people are used to seeing.

Subject identification is also important because it indicates the ways in which the data will be gathered. Will surveys or questionnaires be necessary? Will focus groups or case studies be required? Will the research be quantitative or qualitative? These questions can be answered once the subject has been identified. The goal is to establish research that will identify a point that can be used to measure current standing and improvement.

2. Identify comparative sources

When evaluating aspects of organizations, it is important to compare them against appropriate benchmarks. Once the ways for gathering data have been identified, the sources used for comparison need to be determined.

This starts by asking questions. Are these sources going to be internal or external? Are they homogeneous or heterogeneous? Once these questions are answered, the sources for benchmarking can be determined and selected.

Organizations selecting benchmarks need to be careful to avoid choosing comparative sources based on bias or personal preference. For example, the president of a company might not like a competitor, so he refuses to use that organization as a benchmark. Along the same lines, another president might have a friend who runs a similar company, so she decides to use that friend's organization as a benchmark. Either way, the workplace undergoing the benchmarking process will not reach its potential in terms of improvement because the best sources for comparison were not selected.

3. Collect data

This is the step where the information used to make comparisons is gathered. The comparative sources selected are measured (using surveys, focus groups, etc.) for their best practices.

The data collected depends on the area in the organization that needs to be improved. The following are a few examples of areas that need improvement and the type of data that is collected for those areas:

    Products

Information is collected here to compare products. It involves gathering data about the sales, quality, functionality, and performance of similar products chosen as benchmarks.

Services

Information is collected here to compare services. It involves gathering data about the sales, quality, functionality, and performance of similar services chosen as benchmarks.

Quality

Information is collected here to compare products and services. It involves gathering data about the quality of similar products and services chosen as benchmarks.

Sales

Information is collected here to compare organizations. It involves gathering data about the sales and marketing of similar organizations chosen as benchmarks.

Performance

Information is collected here to compare organizations or specific departments of organizations. This involves gathering data about the performance of similar organizations or the departments within those organizations chosen as benchmarks.

Organizations collecting data need to be careful about how they do so. All information should be gathered anonymously to prevent participating individuals from suffering any type of repercussions for the information they divulge.

4. Determine differences

Once the data has been collected, it needs to be analyzed. This analysis shows the best practices of the source(s) used for benchmarking. Those practices are then compared to the organization seeking improvement, and differences are determined. Those differences are then used to establish goals, as shown in the next step.

5. Establish goals

Decisions need to be made after the data is analyzed. The findings must be used to formulate goals to be valuable. Will these goals involve the implementation of change? The answer should be yes because leaders who choose to do nothing risk the growth and survival of their organizations. They can wait until they are forced to change due to declining market share or other negative factors, but action at that point might be too late.

Goals should have a start date and a projected finish date. This puts employees on a schedule with a time frame. That time frame should be adequate for accomplishing the goals, but it also needs to push people to move forward. They need to know that they must complete their tasks for improvement. In other words, there needs to be some sense of urgency to the process.

Goals should also include milestones. Milestones are achievement levels that are that can used to track progress. They also work well for motivation because they indicate a sense of accomplishment.

6. *Develop plan*

Once the goals have been determined, a plan of action needs to be developed. What is the procedure? Who is the leader? Who will be involved? What is the role of everyone involved? Will training be needed? Will additional resources be required? All of these questions should be addressed in a plan that is understood by everyone. Always remember, "those who fail to plan, plan to fail."

7. *Implement plan*

One of the most important aspects of a plan is often given the least amount of attention. That aspect is implementation. Without proper implementation, the plan does not stand a chance of working. Designated people need to take charge and be held accountable for taking the plan from the development to reality. It needs to be "live" to accomplish the designated goals.

8. *Adjust plan*

More often than not, plans do not go exactly as anticipated. Changes need to be made as concepts take root and people get involved. As most experienced planners are well aware, this is not a cut-and-dry process. It is based on trial and error, and every idea for plan modification needs to be considered before being tossed aside.

In terms of making plan adjustments, people's minds must be like parachutes because they will only work if they are open.

9. *Monitor progress*

After plans have been implemented and adjustments have been made, there will be improvements. These improvements show that the benchmarking has paid off. That payoff is a reward for hard work…but it is by no means the end of the process because it can easily be reduced if progress is not monitored.

Management needs to be aware that employees react well to the progress made from new experiences. However, once that newness wears off, employees often revert to their old habits that originally caused the need for benchmarking. They must be monitored so they do not go back to their ineffective ways of doing things.

Monitoring is not necessarily difficult, but it needs to be continuous...and that is where many organizations fall short. Management thinks they have the problem resolved, so they let down their guard. In a relatively short period of time, the gains that took so much effort to produce are wiped out...and the organization is back to where it started.

Leaders of organizations need to be aware of the need for continual examination and evaluation of employees and progress. They do not want to put time and effort into something that eventually fails, and this can be avoided by using monitoring as a preventative measure.

The following is an example using all nine steps of this benchmarking methodology:

Smith Corporation is a company that sells office furniture, and they want to become the biggest distributor in the United States. They hire an outside consulting company that studies their organization and determines that their weakest area for success is online sales.

The consulting company researches online sellers of office furniture for the most successful company. They find that Jackson Office Supply is the top performer, so Jackson is selected as the comparison source.

The consulting company designs a survey that is issued to organizations that are known customers of Jackson Office Supply. The survey taps perceptions of the overall experience of purchasing online office furniture. Questions rate the importance of quality, price, and service, and ask about areas that present problems or need improvement.

The data is collected, and it is found that convenience is the most important aspect of the purchasing process. Buyers do not view office furniture as a large expense or high priority, so they make purchasing decisions based on the service offered by the supplier. Simplicity and ease of purchase results in sales...and Jackson Office Supply is the top performer in this area.

Upon receiving the results of the consulting company's survey, Smith Corporation embarks on a mission to better their customer service. They set a goal to become known as the best online service organization in the furniture industry within five years.

Smith and the consulting company develop a plan with three essential changes to the current online buying process. These changes are as follows:

- Seven additional customer service representatives will be hired to facilitate the online buying process. Specifically, a 24/7 toll-free phone number will be posted on the company website and all affiliate websites. Customers can call this number at any time and get live support for questions regarding the purchase of any office furniture.
- Any item listed on the website will be guaranteed to be in stock or the customer will receive a twenty percent discount.

- Two-day shipping will be guaranteed for all furniture that is purchased or shipping will be free.

The sales manager, human resources manager, and customer service manager are responsible for implementing this plan. The sales manager is charged with making changes to the website that explains the customer service support, stock guarantee, and shipping guarantee. The human resources manager is responsible for hiring the new customer service representatives. The customer service manager is responsible for training all customer service representatives on the changes to company procedures.

The plan must be implemented within six weeks, and adjustments must be made within an additional six weeks. In short, the plan must be running properly within 12 weeks (90 days) or the responsible people will have to explain why this did not happen.

Fortunately, the plan is implemented and running properly within ten weeks. It is working well, and Smith Corporation begins to see improvement. Three months after the implementation, online office furniture sales are up 15 percent from the same period in the previous year. Twelve months after the implantation, online office furniture sales are up 30 percent from the same period in the previous year.

The president of Smith Corporation assigns the monitoring of this benchmarking process to the vice-president. The vice-president must watch to make sure sales continue to increase so the goal of becoming the best online service organization in the furniture industry is achieved within the designated five years. This means that customer service, stock, and shipping programs must remain in effect. In short, the vice-president will make sure that Smith Corporation does not go back to its former way of selling office furniture to online customers.

The above methodology can be utilized to make benchmarking successful. However, some inhibiting factors can present challenges to this procedure, and those factors are discussed in the next section.

Inhibiting factors

Benchmarking is an excellent concept that can produce valuable information. However, it does not always work. This is for a variety of reasons, but the most common factors involved are as follows:

Resources

Benchmarking requires several different resources. People and time are two major resources that some workplaces simply cannot afford to give up. Many employees perform job functions that are critical for the survival of their organizations, and they do not have the time to work on a benchmarking project.

Another resource is expertise. Most organizations do not have employees capable of performing a valid benchmarking study. This type of analysis requires skills that come from training or experience. Without proper knowledge, benchmarking is not possible.

If time and expertise are resources that are not available, then why can't organizations hire external consultants for their benchmarking? This seems like a relatively simple solution, but the cost is a major drawback. Money is something that many organizations do not have in reserve. If cash is an issue, then expenses prevent organizations from undergoing benchmarking processes.

In short, resources are an inhibiting factor of benchmarking. This is especially true for new or small companies that use all of their available resources for everyday activities.

Management commitment

Management commitment is critical for successful benchmarking. This commitment needs to be from start to finish, but this often fails to happen...and that failure leads to an unsuccessful attempt at benchmarking.

The following needs to be remembered regarding management commitment:

Start at the top

Typically management understands that the benchmarking process needs to start at the top of the organizational hierarchy. However, some leaders fail to understand the importance of their initial involvement. They have a few meetings and pass on the responsibilities to lower-level managers. Yes, they were initially involved...but the lower-level employees are not aware of that involvement. These workers only see supervisors who tell them that the benchmarking is about to take place.

Employees need to see top leadership involved if they are expected to understand the importance of benchmarking. In fact, leaders who are not involved can actually impede the process rather than help it.

Continual involvement

This is an error that management makes regularly. They implement the benchmarking and then move on to other job responsibilities. They completely remove themselves from the process and limit their involvement to occasional monitoring of the progress. This does not work because it shows that management has no interest in seeing the benchmarking through to completion. They are not dedicated to the overall process, and that lack of dedication trickles down to the rest of the employees.

Situations where management is not involved often produce poor results...including failed implementation. The benchmarking is then viewed as a failure, and this might not have been the case if management had been committed throughout the process.

Communication

Communication is important for most situations that involve people working together in organizations. They need to understand each other's words and actions to move forward productively.

Not surprisingly, good communication is critical for benchmarking to be effective. People in the organization need to be updated on the status and progress of the project in a clear and concise way so they understand what has been accomplished and what needs to be done.

In short, good communication reduces confusion and conflicts during the benchmarking process. It creates an environment where people can work together and accomplish tasks that lead to the ultimate goal of improvement.

Resistance to change

Virtually all workplaces have employees who are resistant to change. These individuals like doing things the old way, fear extra work, or do not want to leave their comfort zones. Regardless of the reason, they do not like change and try to prevent it.

Employees can be particularly resistant to benchmarking. After all, the goal is improvement...and improvement typically means change. If management does not take action to stop or prevent employee resistance, then benchmarking will not get past the implementation stage.

Benchmarking faces challenges for proper implementation and completion. However, those challenges can be overcome...and successful organizations reap the benefits that result. That being said, some of the benefits that result from successful benchmarking are discussed in the next section.

Benefits

Benchmarking would not be conducted by organizations if there were no advantages to doing it. Some of these advantages are as follows:

Lower costs

Costs are compared to top-performing companies to reduce them. These costs can be related to processes, products, services, or personnel. For example, benchmarking can show that a television manufacturer's product costs are too high because competitors are using robotics in production, so the television manufacturer invests in 20 percent more robotics for their plant.

Higher quality

Quality is compared to top-performing companies to increase it. This quality can be related to processes, products, services, or personnel. For example, benchmarking can show that a toy company is lacking in customer service, so the company hires more customer service representatives.

Increased sales

Sales are compared to top-performing companies to increase them. For example, benchmarking can show that a pet food company is lacking in trade show sales, so the company commits to a 25 percent increase in trade show attendance.

Reduced uncertainty

Management has the ability to confidently make decisions based on performance measurements that result from related benchmarking. For example, benchmarking at a college can indicate online learning does not work well for students in chemistry classes, so a decision is made for the college to stop teaching physics online.

Enhanced decision-making

Management makes decisions without guessing. For example, benchmarking at a grocery store chain indicates customers are looking for gluten free meat products, so a decision is made to reserve a section for gluten-free meat products in every store.

Better innovation and creativity

Management is not afraid to try new ideas or concepts. For example, benchmarking at a window company shows they are lacking in new product sales, so they begin showing more innovative window designs to their customers.

As you can see, there are some excellent benefits for benchmarking. Organizations need to take full advantage of those benefits, and this is best done by improving the overall process. That being said, benchmark improvement is discussed in the next section.

Improving

Virtually everything in organizations can be improved....including benchmarking. The following are some specific ideas for improvement of the benchmarking process:

Plan

Planning is essential for the success of benchmarking. Two major aspects of planning that can be improved include:

Choose the right benchmark

This might seem like a no-brainer. After all, organizations without a benchmark cannot start the process. However, regardless of how elementary this appears, it can be improved upon. Leaders in organizations need to spend considerable time and effort thinking of the best possible benchmarks for their desired accomplishments. This means examining a variety of possibilities and not ruling out any based on preference or bias. Remember, better benchmarks will result in more applicable results.

Involve top management

Managers are expected to be involved in the implementation of any type of change. However, sometimes they are not sure of their roles...just like the rest of the employees. Leadership in organizations needs to make managers fully aware of their roles so they can help implement the benchmarking rather than become a barrier.

Minimize resistance

Most people understand that employee resistance needs to be minimized for any type of organizational change....including benchmarking. However, a method for doing this needs to be determined.

A roadmap should be developed that provides structure and goals so employees understand everything about the benchmarking. This eliminates the fear of the unknown and helps workers accept the change and begin the process.

Specific elements of a roadmap include:

The reason for the benchmarking

This is often the most important aspect of the roadmap. Employees need to know why benchmarking is taking place so they can justify it in their own minds. Organizations that do not provide logical reasons for this are "shooting themselves in the foot" before that benchmarking has a chance to take root.

The procedure for the benchmarking

This provides direction so employees are not left wondering about the next step in the process. Procedures are important because they provide structure and prevent unnecessary stress worrying about the course of action.

The time frame for the benchmarking

Time frames serve two functions. First, they help employees organize their thoughts and actions regarding the benchmarking. This allows for prioritizing the most important tasks. Second, they establish deadlines so workers understand time expectations. Deadlines can be modified later on, but they provide a starting point for completion.

The employees' role in the benchmarking

Employees need to know what they are expected to do for benchmarking to be properly implemented. Employees who understand their roles will help with the implementation process by eliminating confusion.

The goal(s) of the benchmarking

Roadmaps need to indicate the point at which the benchmarking is considered successful, and this is done by establishing goals. Goals let employees know what needs to be accomplished, and they keep them from questioning the objectives of the benchmarking.

Validate data

Make sure the data collected is comprehensive, concise, and accurate. Comparisons and evaluations based on this information are used to formulate conclusions that will be inaccurate if the data is not valid. Always think about the fact that the data determines strengths and weaknesses, and it leads to recommendations for improvement. That improvement will not be beneficial if it is derived from erroneous information.

Clarify results

This essentially involves the reporting of findings. Results need to be reported in a way that is understood by everyone involved. Unfortunately, this is not always done because people present their findings as if they were being published in academic journals. When this happens, results are only understood by a select few individuals because the real meaning is distorted by the wording.

Implement findings

Some organizations effectively move through the benchmarking process until they get to the recommendations...and this is where their effectiveness ends. This happens because it is painful to implement some of the changes necessary for improvement. For example, it is much easier to focus on strengths and ignore weaknesses. However, weaknesses need to be addressed to get the most benefit from benchmarking. In short, addressing strengths and weaknesses improves the value of benchmarking to organizations.

Monitor progress

As noted earlier in this book, the hardest part about monitoring the progress of benchmarking is doing it continuously. Continuous monitoring prevents gains from lessening or disappearing, and it helps organizations progressively get better.

An argument can be made that continuous monitoring is the best method of improvement because, without it, benchmarking can be rendered useless. If this happens, then the amount of time and effort spent getting to the monitoring stage are completely wasted.

Summary

Benchmarking is beneficial for organizations. It can be challenging to implement and follow-through, but the results are useful for bettering workplaces through goal attainment and continuous improvement. This helps organizations grow and prosper as they compete in ever-changing markets.

The book explores the following:

- Types of benchmarking
- Methodology of benchmarking
- Inhibiting factors of benchmarking
- Benefits of benchmarking
- Improving benchmarking

Congratulations! You now understand more about benchmarking...an important driver of the organizational change needed for improvement.

Manufactured by Amazon.ca
Acheson, AB